Pasta Salad Recipes For The Home Cook

Sadie .B Woods

All rights reserved. Copyright © 2023 Sadie .B Woods

COPYRIGHT © 2023 Sadie .B Woods

All rights reserved.

No part of this book must be reproduced, stored in a retrieval system, or shared by any means, electronic, mechanical, photocopying, recording, or otherwise, without written permission from the publisher.

Every precaution has been taken in the preparation of this book; still the publisher and author assume no responsibility for errors or omissions. Nor do they assume any liability for damages resulting from the use of the information contained herein.

Legal Notice:

This book is copyright protected and is only meant for your individual use. You are not allowed to amend, distribute, sell, use, quote or paraphrase any of its part without the written consent of the author or publisher.

Introduction

This book presents a delightful array of pasta-based dishes that capture the essence of Southern comfort cuisine while offering simplicity and flavor in every bite.

The cookbook kicks off with a versatile Basic Pasta Casserole Recipe, setting the stage for a culinary journey through Southern-inspired pasta creations. From there, readers are treated to a variety of mouthwatering pasta casseroles that showcase classic Southern ingredients and flavors.

Traditional favorites like White Lasagna Casserole and Simple Egg Noodle Lasagna Bake offer comforting layers of pasta, cheese, and savory fillings, perfect for family dinners or casual gatherings. Meanwhile, Mexican-inspired dishes such as Mexican Lasagna Casserole and Mexican Stuffed Shells Bake add a spicy twist to traditional pasta recipes, infusing them with vibrant flavors and bold spices.

For those seeking hearty and satisfying meals, options like Spicy Beef Casserole Bake and Beef Macaroni Skillet provide wholesome dishes that are both delicious and filling. Italian-inspired offerings such as Italiano Pasta Casserole and Italian Sausage Lasagna Casserole showcase the rich flavors of herbs, cheeses, and sauces that are synonymous with Southern Italian cooking.

The cookbook also features a selection of pasta skillet dinners and noodle bakes that are quick and easy to prepare, making them ideal for busy weeknights. From the Creamy Ground Beef Casserole to the Taco Noodle Bake, these recipes offer convenient solutions for satisfying hunger with minimal effort.

For those looking to incorporate more variety into their pasta repertoire, the cookbook includes recipes featuring other proteins such as pork, chicken, and shrimp. From the Overnight Pork Spaghetti Bake to the Shrimp Pasta Medley, these dishes offer a delicious departure from traditional pasta fare while maintaining the Southern flair that defines the cookbook.

To round out the culinary experience, the cookbook includes a selection of pasta salads that are perfect for picnics, potlucks, or light meals. From the Hearty Macaroni Salad to the Ham Pecan Blue Cheese Pasta Salad, these refreshing dishes offer a delightful balance of flavors and textures that are sure to please any palate.

With its wide range of recipes and Southern-inspired flavors, this book is a must-have resource for pasta lovers looking to infuse their meals with a touch of Southern charm and hospitality. Whether you're a seasoned cook or just starting out in the kitchen, this cookbook offers something for everyone to enjoy.

Contents

Basic Pasta Casserole Recipe 1

White Lasagna Casserole 3

Mexican Lasagna Casserole 5

Seashell Provolone Casserole 7

Simple Egg Noodle LasagnaBake 9

Meat Sauce Linguine Casserole 11

Zucchini Lasagna Bake 13

Spicy Beef Casserole Bake 15

Beef Macaroni Skillet 17

Italiano Pasta Casserole 18

Mexican Stuffed Shells Bake 20

Mexican Casserole 22

Spaghetti Casserole 24

Beefy Noodle Skillet Dinner 26

Baked Rotini Casserole 27

Chili Noodle Dinner 29

Hamburger Noodle Bake 30

Taco Noodle Bake 32

Creamy Ground Beef Casserole 34

Classic Pastitsio 36

Choose A Flavor Macaroni andCheese Casserole 38

Overnight Pork Spaghetti Bake 40

Skillet Sausage PenneCasserole 42

Sausage Noodle Casserole 44

Chorizo Sausage Casserole 46

Eggplant Sausage Casserole 48

Pizza Pasta Bake 50
Pork and Noodle Bake 52
Cheesy Pork Casserole 54
Pork Noodle Skillet 56
Italian Sausage Lasagna Casserole 58
Ham Noodle Skillet 60
Ham Cheddar Casserole 61
Spaghetti Ham Casserole 63
Creamy Ham Medley 65
Chicken Ham Noodle Casserole 66
Cream Cheese Ham Casserole 67
Creamy Ham & Chicken Lasagna Bake 69
Sesame Chicken Noodle Bake 71
Chicken Asparagus Pasta Supper 73
Cheesy Chicken Enchilada Skillet 75
Chicken Pasta Broccoli Bake 76
Chicken Linguine Casserole 78
Chicken, Tomato & Sausage Skillet 80
Chicken Macaroni Bake 82
Spinach Chicken Noodle Bake 83
Smoked Sausage Noodle Bake 85
Smoked Sausage Vegetable Pasta Skillet 86
Smoked Sausage Broccoli Skillet 88
Banquet Stroganoff 90
Frankaroni Potluck Casserole 92
Bacon Spaghetti 94
Cabbage Bacon Noodle Casserole 95
Gorgonzola Bacon Mac & Cheese Bake 96
Parmesan Turkey Broccoli Casserole 98

Turkey Tomato Casserole	100
Ham and Turkey Spaghetti Casserole	102
Turkey Noodle Bake	104
Turkey Stroganoff Casserole	106
Leftover Turkey Casserole	108
Hot Brown Pasta Casserole	109
Turkey Olive Casserole	110
Chicken Lasagna Bake	111
Chicken Spaghetti Casserole	113
Chicken Vegetable Spaghetti Casserole	115
Chicken Superb Casserole	117
Pesto Chicken and Pasta Casserole	119
Szechuan Noodle Skillet	121
Roasted Pepper & Broccoli Pasta Skillet	123
Overnight Macaroni & Chicken Casserole	124
Oven Baked Shrimp Stroganoff	125
Seafood Manicotti Casserole	126
Crab Meat Lasagna	128
Shrimp Noodle Casserole	130
Shrimp Feta Vermicelli	132
Scalloped Oyster Macaroni Casserole	134
Crawfish Pasta Casserole	136
Three Cheese Ziti Casserole	138
Four Cheese Pasta Bake	139
Cheesy Macaroni Mushroom Bake	141
Vegetable Lasagna Casserole	143
Veggie Macaroni Cheese Casserole	145
Vegetable Noodle Casserole	147
Avocado Vegetable Lasagna Casserole	149

Four Cheese Noodle Casserole	151
Baked Summer Veggie Ziti Casserole	152
Macaroni, Cheese & Tomato Casserole	154
Garden Primavera Skillet	155
Red Bell Pepper Pasta Bake	157
Sauteed Spaghetti Vegetable Skillet	159
Asparagus Spaghetti Casserole	161
Cheddar Onion Macaroni Casserole	163
Southwestern Pumpkin Stuffed Shells	164
Spinach Stuffed Shells	166
Spinach Manicotti Casserole	168
Spinach Macaroni Bake	170
Blue Cheese Macaroni Bake	172
Monterey Jack Macaroni Bake	174
Turkey Picante Noodle Casserole	176
Plentiful Pasta & Black Eye Pea Salad	178
Garden Macaroni Salad	180
Asparagus Pasta Salad	181
Garden Tortellini Salad	182
Southwestern Pasta Salad	184
Tossed Shell Salad	185
Cabbage Slaw Pasta Salad	186
Confetti Orzo Pasta Salad	187
Linguine Vegetable Pasta Salad	189
Broccoli Cauliflower Pasta Salad	190
Pistachio Pasta Salad	192
Macaroni and Cheese Salad	194
Pasta Bean Salad	195
Pasta Basil Toss	196

Caesar Presto Pasta Salad	197
Caesar Ravioli Salad	198
Green Bean Pasta Salad	199
Vegetable Pasta Salad	200
Oriental Pasta Salad	202
Ratatouille Pasta Salad	203
Vinaigrette Pasta VegetableSalad	205
Water Chestnut Pasta Salad	207
Garden Pasta Medley	208
Artichoke Salami Pasta Salad	209
Deli Style Macaroni Salad	211
Dilled Macaroni Salad	212
Tomato Olive Pasta Salad	213
Spinach Dijon Pasta Salad	214
Artichoke Hearts Pasta	216
Ramen Noodle Salad	217
Gourmet Macaroni Salad	218
Parmesan Artichoke Salad	219
Tortellini Salad	220
Tarragon Vegetable Pasta Salad	222
Spicy Beef Pasta Salad	223
Chicken Spaghetti Salad	225
Dilled Chicken Macaroni Salad	226
Fruited Pasta Salad	227
Luncheon Pasta Salad	229
Chicken Pasta Salad	230
Tarragon Pasta Chicken Salad	232
Chicken Tortellini Salad	234
Ranch Turkey & Pasta Salad	236

Confetti Tuna Salad	237
Gourmet Tuna Pasta Salad	238
Tuna Macaroni Salad	240
Stuffed Tomato with Tuna PastaSalad	241
Whole Wheat Tuna MacaroniSalad	243
Tuna Vegetable Pasta Salad	245
Salmon and Macaroni Salad	247
Crab Meat Macaroni Salad	248
Crab Meat Shrimp Pasta Salad	249
Shrimp Delight Salad	251
Shrimp Pasta Medley	253
Hearty Macaroni Salad	255
Ham Dijon Pasta Salad	256
Italian Pasta Vinaigrette	257
Kid Pleasing Ham Pasta Salad	258
Ranch Macaroni VegetableSalad	259
Ham Pecan Blue Cheese PastaSalad	260
Rotini Salad	261

Basic Pasta Casserole Recipe

Makes 6 servings or a 11 x 7 casserole dish. Bake at 350° or until the pasta is done and the casserole hot and bubbly.

This is a casserole recipe that I use when I have an abundance of leftovers and need to fix dinner. Use this basic casserole recipe and ingredients you have on hand to create your own unique casserole. You may just find your family loves your new creation.

Basic casserole recipe: Sauce mix, meat, pasta, vegetable, casserole extras and one or two toppings.

Sauce mix: 1 can cream of mushroom, chicken or celery soup, 1 cup sour cream, 1 cup whole milk, 1 teaspoon salt and 1 teaspoon black pepper. Stir until combined. You can substitute plain yogurt for the sour cream if desired.

You can substitute a 29 oz. can crushed or diced tomatoes with juice in place of the soup, sour cream and milk in the sauce mix if desired. Try the flavored tomatoes such as Italian seasoned tomatoes, Mexican style tomatoes, garlic tomatoes, etc. The tomatoes provide a unique twist to casseroles.

Meat: Use 2-3 cups of your favorite cooked meat. Add the sauce mix desired to flavor the meat.

Vegetable: Frozen or canned vegetables make casseroles easy. Use a 10 oz. pkg. frozen vegetable of choice or 15 oz. can vegetable of your choice drained.

Pasta: 2 cups uncooked elbow macaroni, 4 cups uncooked egg noodles or 3 cups uncooked shell pasta. Cook the pasta before adding to the casserole.

Toppings: 1/2 cup of your favorite shredded cheese, breadcrumbs or canned fried onions.

Extras: Add one or more of the following extras to your casserole. Use 1/2 to 1 cup vegetables if desired. Our favorites vegetables are cooked mushrooms, sliced black olives, chopped red, green or yellow bell peppers, chopped onions or celery. Additional extras that are great in casseroles are 2 minced garlic cloves, 4 oz. can chopped green chiles or a package of taco or chili seasoning mix. You can use as many extras as you like.

White Lasagna Casserole

Makes 6 servings

Ingredients

1 lb. ground beef
1/2 lb. ground pork sausage
1 cup chopped onion
1/2 cup chopped celery
1 garlic clove, minced
2 tsp. dried basil
1 tsp. dried oregano
1/2 tsp. dried Italian seasoning
1/2 tsp. salt
1 cup whole milk
3 oz. pkg. cream cheese, softened
1/2 cup chicken broth
8 oz. egg noodles
2 cups shredded cheddar cheese
1 1/2 cups shredded Gouda cheese
12 oz. carton cottage cheese
1 egg, beaten
2 cups shredded mozzarella cheese

Directions

In a skillet over medium heat, add the ground beef, pork sausage, onion, celery and garlic. Stir the meats frequently so they break into crumbles as they cook. Cook about 8 minutes or until the ground beef and sausage are well browned and no longer pink. Drain all the grease from the skillet. Add the basil, oregano, Italian seasoning, salt, milk, cream cheese and chicken broth. Stir until well combined. Bring to a boil and simmer for 3 minutes.

While the meat is cooking, cook the egg noodles. In a large sauce pan over medium heat, add 2 quarts water. Bring the water to a boil and add the egg noodles. Boil for 6-7 minutes or until the noodles are tender. Remove the pan from the heat and drain all the water from the noodles.

In a mixing bowl, add the cheddar cheese, Gouda cheese, cottage cheese and egg. Stir until well combined. Add the noodles and toss until combined. Preheat the oven to 350°. Spray a 9 x 13 casserole dish with non stick cooking spray. Add the noodles to the casserole dish. Spoon the meat sauce over the noodles. Lightly toss until combined. Sprinkle the mozzarella cheese over the top.

Cover the dish with aluminum foil or a lid. Bake for 40 minutes or until the casserole is hot and bubbly. Remove the dish from the oven and serve.

Mexican Lasagna Casserole

Makes 8 servings

Ingredients

8 oz. egg noodles
8 oz. ground pork sausage
8 oz. ground beef
15 oz. can ranch style pinto beans, drained
2/3 cup canned diced tomatoes with green chiles
1 tsp. garlic powder
1 tsp. ground cumin
1/2 tsp. salt
1/2 tsp. black pepper
10.75 oz. can cream of celery soup
10.75 oz. can cream of mushroom soup
10 oz. can enchilada sauce
2 cups shredded sharp cheddar cheese
1 cup shredded Monterey Jack cheese
1 tomato, diced
4 chopped green onions
1/4 cup chopped fresh cilantro
1 avocado, chopped

Directions

In a large sauce pan over medium heat, add 10 cups water. Bring the water to a boil and add the egg noodles. Boil for 6-7 minutes or until the noodles are tender. Remove the pan from the heat and drain all the water from the noodles.

In a large skillet over medium heat, add the pork sausage and ground beef. Stir frequently to break the meats into crumbles as it cooks. Cook about 8 minutes or until the meats are well browned and no longer pink. Drain off the excess grease. Add the pinto beans, tomatoes with green chiles, garlic powder, cumin, salt, black pepper, cream of celery soup, cream of mushroom soup and enchilada sauce. Stir constantly and bring the sauce to a boil. Reduce the heat to low and simmer for 5 minutes. Remove the skillet from the heat.

Preheat the oven to 350°. Spray a 9 x 13 casserole dish with non stick cooking spray. Place 1/2 the noodles in the bottom of the casserole dish. Spoon half the meat sauce over the noodles. Sprinkle 1 cup cheddar cheese over the sauce. Repeat the layering process 1 more time. Sprinkle the Monterey Jack cheese over the top. Cover the dish with aluminum foil. Bake for 45 minutes or until hot and bubbly.

Remove the dish from the oven and cool for 5 minutes before removing the aluminum foil. Remove the aluminum foil and sprinkle the tomato, green onions, cilantro and avocado over the top before serving.

Seashell Provolone Casserole

Makes 12 servings

Ingredients

3 onions, finely chopped
1/4 cup unsalted butter, melted
2 lbs. ground beef
15 oz. jar spaghetti sauce
16 oz. can stewed tomatoes
1 cup sliced cooked mushrooms
1 tsp. garlic salt
8 oz. pkg. small shell macaroni
8 oz. sliced provolone cheese
3 cups sour cream
1 cup shredded mozzarella cheese

Directions

In a large skillet over medium heat, add the onions and butter. Saute for 4 minutes. Add the ground beef to the skillet. Stir frequently to break the meat into crumbles as it cooks. Cook about 8-10 minutes or until the ground beef is browned and no longer pink. Drain off the excess grease. Add the spaghetti sauce, tomatoes with juice, mushrooms and garlic salt. Stir until well combined. Simmer for 20 minutes. Remove the skillet from the heat.

While the meat sauce is cooking, cook the macaroni. In a large sauce pan over medium heat, add 8 cups water. Bring the water to a boil and add the macaroni. Boil for 6-7 minutes or until the macaroni is tender. Remove the pan from the heat and drain all the water from the macaroni.

Preheat the oven to 350°. Spray a deep 4 quart casserole dish with non stick cooking spray. Spread half the macaroni in the bottom of the casserole dish. Spoon half the meat sauce over the noodles. Lay half the provolone slices over the meat sauce. Spread half the sour cream over the provolone cheese.

Repeat the layering process one more time. Sprinkle the mozzarella cheese over the top. Cover the dish with aluminum foil or a lid. Bake for 30 minutes. Remove the aluminum foil and bake for 15 minutes or until hot, bubbly and the cheeses are melted. Remove the casserole from the oven and cool for 10 minutes before serving.

Simple Egg Noodle Lasagna Bake

Makes 6 servings

Ingredients

4 oz. egg noodles
8 oz. pkg. cream cheese, softened
1 cup cottage cheese
1/2 cup sour cream
1 lb. ground chuck
14 oz. jar spaghetti sauce
1/2 cup grated Parmesan cheese

Directions

In a large sauce pan over medium heat, add 8 cups water. Bring the water to a boil and add the egg noodles. Boil for 6-7 minutes or until the noodles are tender. Remove the pan from the heat and drain all the water from the noodles.

In a mixing bowl, add the cream cheese, cottage cheese and sour cream. Stir until well combined. In a skillet over medium heat, add the ground chuck. Stir frequently to break the meat into crumbles as it cooks. Cook for 8 minutes or until the ground chuck is well browned and no longer pink. Drain off any excess grease. Add the spaghetti sauce and mix until combined.

Preheat the oven to 350°. Spray a 2 quart casserole dish with non stick cooking spray. Add the noodles to the casserole dish. Spread the cream cheese sauce over the noodles. Spoon the ground beef sauce over the cheese sauce. Sprinkle the Parmesan cheese over the top. Cover the dish with aluminum foil or a lid. Bake for 35-45 minutes or until the casserole is hot and bubbly. Remove the dish from the oven and cool for 5 minutes before serving.

Meat Sauce Linguine Casserole

Makes 8 servings

Ingredients

2 lbs. lean ground beef
2 garlic cloves, minced
28 oz. can crushed tomatoes
8 oz. can tomato sauce
6 oz. can tomato paste
2 tsp. granulated sugar
8 oz. linguine noodles
16 oz. container sour cream
8 oz. pkg. cream cheese, softened
8 green onions, chopped
2 cups shredded cheddar cheese

Directions

In a large skillet over medium heat, add the ground beef and garlic. Stir frequently to break the meat into crumbles as it cooks. Cook about 8 minutes or until the ground beef is well browned and no longer pink. Drain off the excess grease.

Add the crushed tomatoes, tomato sauce, tomato paste and granulated sugar to the skillet. Stir until well combined. Bring the sauce to a boil and reduce the heat to low. Simmer for 30 minutes. Remove the skillet from the heat.

While the sauce is cooking, cook the linguine. In a large sauce pan over medium heat, add 10 cups water. Bring the water to a boil and add the linguine noodles. Boil for 6-7 minutes or until the linguine is tender. Remove the pan from the heat and drain all the water from the noodles.

In a mixing bowl, add the sour cream, cream cheese and green onions. Stir until well combined. Preheat the oven to 350°. Spray a 9 x 13 casserole dish with non stick cooking spray. Spread the linguine noodles in the bottom of the casserole dish. Spread the sour cream sauce over the noodles. Pour the meat sauce over the sour cream sauce.

Bake for 25 minutes or until the casserole is hot and bubbly. Sprinkle the cheddar cheese over the top. Bake for 10 minutes. Remove the dish from the oven and cool for 5 minutes before serving.

Zucchini Lasagna Bake

Makes 8 servings

Ingredients

1 lb. ground beef
4 cups shredded zucchini
3/4 cup chopped onion
2 garlic cloves, minced
14 oz. can stewed tomatoes
2 cups water
12 oz. can tomato paste
1 tbs. minced fresh parsley
1 1/2 tsp. salt
1 tsp. granulated sugar
1/2 tsp. dried oregano
1/2 tsp. black pepper
8 oz. rotini pasta
15 oz. carton ricotta cheese
2 cups shredded mozzarella cheese
1 cup grated Parmesan cheese

Directions

In a large skillet over medium heat, add the ground beef, zucchini, onion and garlic. Stir frequently to break the ground beef into crumbles as it cooks. Cook about 8 minutes or until the ground beef is well browned and no longer pink. Drain off the excess grease.

Add the stewed tomatoes with juice, water, tomato paste, parsley, salt, granulated sugar, oregano and black pepper. Stir until well combined and bring the sauce to a boil. Reduce the heat to low and simmer the sauce about 30 minutes or until thickened. Remove the skillet from the heat.

While the sauce is cooking, make the pasta. In a large sauce pan over medium heat, add 10 cups water. Bring the water to a boil and add the rotini pasta. Boil for 6-7 minutes or until the pasta is tender. Remove the pan from the heat and drain all the water from the rotini pasta.

In a mixing bowl, add the ricotta cheese and mozzarella cheese. Stir until combined. Preheat the oven to 350°. Spray a 9 x 13 casserole dish with non stick cooking spray. Spread 1 cup ground beef sauce in the bottom of the casserole dish. Spread half the rotini pasta over the sauce. Spoon half of the remaining ground beef sauce over the noodles. Spread half the ricotta mixture over the sauce.

Repeat the layering process one more time. Sprinkle the Parmesan cheese over the top of the casserole. Cover the dish with aluminum foil. Bake for 45 minutes or until the casserole is hot and bubbly. Remove the aluminum foil and bake for 10 minutes or until the Parmesan cheese is lightly browned. Remove the dish from the oven and cool for 10 minutes before serving.

Spicy Beef Casserole Bake

Makes 8 servings

Ingredients

1 lb. ground beef
14 oz. can diced tomatoes
10 oz. can diced tomatoes with green chiles
2 tsp. granulated sugar
2 tsp. salt
1/4 tsp. cayenne pepper
6 oz. can tomato paste
6 drops Tabasco sauce
1 bay leaf
6 oz. pkg. egg noodles
6 green onions, chopped
1 cup sour cream
1 cup shredded sharp cheddar cheese
1 cup shredded Parmesan cheese
1 cup shredded mozzarella cheese

Directions

In a large skillet over medium heat, add the ground beef. Stir frequently to break the meat into crumbles as it cooks. Cook about 8 minutes or until the ground beef is well browned and no longer pink. Drain the grease from the skillet.

Add the diced tomatoes with juice, tomatoes with green chiles, granulated sugar, salt, cayenne pepper, tomato paste, Tabasco sauce and bay leaf to the skillet. Stir until well combined. Bring the sauce to a boil and reduce the heat to low. Place a lid on the skillet and simmer the sauce for 15 minutes. Remove the skillet from the heat.

While the sauce is cooking, make the egg noodles. In a large sauce pan over medium heat, add 8 cups water. Bring the water to a boil and add the egg noodles. Boil for 6-7 minutes or until the noodles are tender. Remove the pan from the heat and drain all the water from the noodles. Add the green onions, sour cream, cheddar cheese and Parmesan cheese to the hot noodles. Toss until combined.

Preheat the oven to 350°. Spray a 9 x 13 casserole dish with non stick cooking spray. Spread half the noodles in the bottom of the dish. Spread half the ground beef sauce over the noodles. Repeat the layering process 1 more time. Sprinkle the mozzarella cheese over the top of the casserole.

Cover the dish with aluminum foil. Bake for 40 minutes. Remove the aluminum foil and bake for 10 minutes or until the dish is hot and bubbly. Remove from the oven and cool for 10 minutes before serving.

Beef Macaroni Skillet

I have used this recipe on a busy day more times than I can remember. Keep the ingredients on hand for a quick dinner.

Makes 4 servings

Ingredients

1 lb. ground chuck
1 1/4 cups water
1 pkg. onion gravy mix
8 oz. can tomato sauce
1 cup elbow macaroni
1 cup shredded Mozzarella cheese

Directions

In a skillet over medium heat, add the ground chuck. Stir frequently to break the meat into crumbles as it cooks. Cook about 8 minutes or until the ground chuck is well browned and no longer pink. Drain off the excess grease.

Add the water, onion gravy mix and tomato sauce to the skillet. Stir until well combined and bring to a boil. Add the elbow macaroni. Stir until combined. Place a lid on the skillet and cook about 10 minutes or until the macaroni is tender. Remove the skillet from the heat and sprinkle the mozzarella cheese over the top before serving.

Italiano Pasta Casserole

Makes 6 servings

Ingredients

15 oz. container ricotta cheese
1 egg, beaten
2 tsp. garlic powder
14 jumbo pasta shells, cooked
1 lb. lean ground beef
1 onion, chopped
2 garlic cloves, minced
28 oz. can diced tomatoes
2 cups sliced fresh mushrooms
1 tbs. fresh chopped parsley
1 tsp. salt
1 tsp. Italian seasoning
15 oz. can tomato sauce
1/2 cup grated Parmesan cheese

Directions

Spray a 11 x 7 baking dish with non stick cooking spray. In a mixing bowl, add the ricotta cheese, egg and garlic powder. Stir until well combined. Fill the cooked pasta shells with the ricotta filling. Place the shells in the prepared baking dish.

In a skillet over medium heat, add the ground beef, onion and garlic. Stir frequently to break the meat into crumbles as it cooks. Cook about 8 minutes or until the ground beef is well browned and no longer pink. Drain off the excess grease.

Add the tomatoes with juice, mushrooms, parsley, salt and Italian seasoning. Stir frequently and simmer for 10 minutes. Stir in the tomato sauce and cook for 3 minutes. Remove the skillet from the heat.

Preheat the oven to 350°. Spoon the ground beef sauce over the shells in the casserole dish. Bake for 20 minutes or until the filling in the pasta shells is hot. Sprinkle the Parmesan cheese over the top and bake for 5 minutes. Remove the dish from the oven and serve.

Mexican Stuffed Shells Bake

Makes 5 servings

Ingredients

20 jumbo pasta shells
16 oz. jar picante sauce
8 oz. can tomato sauce
1/2 cup water
1 lb. ground beef
4 oz. can chopped green chiles
1 cup shredded Monterey Jack cheese
3 oz. can french fried onions

Directions

In a large sauce pan over medium heat, add 10 cups water. Bring the water to a boil and add the pasta shells. Boil for 6-7 minutes or until the shells are tender. Remove the pan from the heat and drain all the water from the shells. Do not over cook the shells. They need to be tender but firm when ready.

In a mixing bowl, add the picante sauce, tomato sauce and water. Stir until well combined. In a skillet over medium heat, add the ground beef. Stir frequently to break the meat into crumbles as it cooks. Cook for 7 minutes or until the ground beef is well browned and no longer pink. Drain off the excess grease.

Add 1/2 cup picante sauce mixture, green chiles, 1/2 cup Monterey Jack cheese and 1/2 the fried onions to the ground beef. Stir until well combined and thoroughly heated. Remove the skillet from the heat.

Preheat the oven to 350°. Fill the pasta shells with the ground beef filling. Spread half of the remaining picante sauce mixture in a 9 x 13 baking dish. Place the filled shells on the sauce. Spoon the remaining sauce over the shells. Cover the dish with aluminum foil or a lid. Bake for 30 minutes. Remove the aluminum foil and sprinkle 1/2 cup Monterey Jack cheese and the remaining fried onions over the top of the shells. Bake for 10 minutes. Remove the dish from the oven and serve.

Mexican Casserole

Makes 6 servings

Ingredients

1 cup elbow macaroni
1 lb. ground beef
1/4 cup chopped onion
15 oz. can Mexican style chili beans
10 oz. can enchilada sauce
3 tsp. chili powder
1/2 tsp. salt
1/4 tsp. black pepper
1 cup shredded cheddar cheese
3/4 cup crushed corn chips

Directions

In a large sauce pan over medium heat, add 8 cups water. Bring the water to a boil and add the macaroni. Boil for 6-7 minutes or until the macaroni is tender. Remove the pan from the heat and drain all the water from the macaroni.

In a skillet over medium heat, add the ground beef and onion. Stir frequently to break the meat into crumbles as it cooks. Cook about 7 minutes or until the ground beef is well browned and no longer pink. Remove the skillet from the heat and drain off the excess grease.

Add the chili beans, enchilada sauce, chili powder, salt, black pepper and macaroni to the ground beef. Stir until combined. Preheat the oven to 350°. Spray a 2 quart casserole dish with non stick cooking spray. Spoon the ground beef filling into the casserole dish. Sprinkle the cheddar cheese and corn chips over the top of the casserole.

Bake for 30 minutes or until the casserole is hot, bubbly and golden brown on top. Remove the dish from the oven and serve.

Spaghetti Casserole

Makes 6 servings

Ingredients

8 oz. pkg. thin spaghetti noodles
1 lb. ground beef
1/2 cup chopped green bell pepper
1 large onion, chopped
10.75 oz. can condensed tomato soup
2/3 cup water
8 oz. can whole kernel corn, drained
1/2 cup sliced black olives
2 cups shredded cheddar cheese
1/2 tsp. salt
1 1/2 tsp. dried Italian seasoning

Directions

In a large sauce pan over medium heat, add 10 cups water. Bring the water to a boil and add the noodles. Boil for 6-7 minutes or until the noodles are tender. Remove the pan from the heat and drain all the water from the pasta.

In a large skillet over medium heat, add the ground beef, green bell pepper and onion. Stir frequently to break the meat into crumbles as it cooks. Cook about 8 minutes or until the ground beef is well browned and no longer pink. Drain the excess grease from the skillet. Add the tomato soup, 2/3 cup water, corn, black olives, cheddar cheese, noodles, salt and Italian seasoning. Stir until well combined and cook only until thoroughly heated. Remove the skillet from the heat.

Spoon the casserole into a 9 x 13 baking dish. At this point, you can cover the casserole and refrigerate overnight if desired or bake right away. Make this casserole the night before and you only have to bake the casserole before serving. I think most casseroles taste better if left to sit refrigerated overnight. The flavors blend and they taste extra delicious.

To bake the casserole when prepared, preheat the oven to 350°. Bake for 30 minutes or until the casserole is hot and bubbly. If the casserole is refrigerated, let the casserole sit for 30 minutes at room temperature before baking. Bake for 30-40 minutes or until the casserole is hot and bubbly.

Beefy Noodle Skillet Dinner

Makes 4 servings

Ingredients

1/2 lb. ground beef
1 onion, chopped
1 garlic clove, minced
3 tbs. minced fresh parsley
6 oz. can tomato paste
2 1/4 cups water
1 tsp. granulated sugar
3/4 tsp. salt
2 cups egg noodles
1/4 cup grated Parmesan cheese

Directions

In a large skillet over medium heat, add the ground beef, onion and garlic. Stir frequently to break the meat into crumbles as it cooks. Cook about 8 minutes or until the ground beef is done and no longer pink. Drain off the excess grease.

Add the parsley, tomato paste, water, granulated sugar and salt to the skillet. Stir until well combined. Reduce the heat to low and simmer for 10 minutes. Add the eggs noodles and stir until combined. Place a lid on the skillet. Simmer for 15 minutes or until the noodles are tender. Remove the skillet from the heat and sprinkle the Parmesan cheese over the top before serving.

Baked Rotini Casserole

Makes 8 servings

Ingredients

1 lb. ground beef
1 onion, chopped
1 green bell pepper, chopped
28 oz. can crushed tomatoes
6 oz. can tomato paste
1 cup cooked sliced mushrooms
1 tsp. salt
1/2 tsp. dried basil
1/4 tsp. garlic powder
1/4 tsp. dried oregano
1/4 tsp. dried red pepper flakes, crushed
8 oz. rotini pasta, cooked
3 cups shredded mozzarella cheese

Directions

In a large skillet over medium heat, add the ground beef, onion and green bell pepper. Stir frequently to break the meat into crumbles as it cooks. Cook about 8 minutes or until the ground beef is well browned and no longer pink. Drain off the excess grease.

Add the crushed tomatoes, tomato paste, mushrooms, salt, basil, garlic powder, oregano and red pepper flakes. Stir until combined and simmer for 10 minutes. Remove the skillet from the heat.

Preheat the oven to 350°. Spray a 9 x 13 casserole dish with non stick cooking spray. Add the rotini pasta, mozzarella cheese and ground beef sauce to the casserole dish. Stir until well combined.

Bake for 30 minutes or until the dish is hot, bubbly and the cheese melted. Remove the dish from the oven and serve.

Chili Noodle Dinner

Makes 12 servings

Ingredients

3 lbs. ground beef
1 onion, chopped
2 pkgs. chili seasoning mix
5 oz. pkg. egg noodles
46 oz. can tomato juice
2 cans chili beans, 15 oz. size
1 tbs. Worcestershire sauce
1/2 tsp. garlic salt
1/2 tsp. onion salt
1/4 tsp. black pepper

Directions

In a dutch oven, add the ground beef and onion. Stir frequently to break the meat into crumbles as it cooks. Cook for 10 minutes or until the ground beef is well browned and no longer pink. Drain off the excess grease.

Add the chili seasoning mix, egg noodles, tomato juice, chili beans, Worcestershire sauce, garlic salt, onion salt and black pepper. Stir until well combined. Bring the chili to a boil and reduce the heat to low. Place a lid on the dutch oven and simmer for 1 hour. Stir occasionally while cooking. Remove the pan from the heat and serve.

Hamburger Noodle Bake

Makes 8 servings

Ingredients

1 lb. ground beef
15 oz. can diced tomatoes
2 tsp. granulated sugar
1 tsp. salt
8 oz. can tomato sauce
5 oz. pkg. egg noodles
3 oz. pkg. cream cheese, cubed
1 cup sour cream
6 green onions, chopped
1/2 cup shredded cheddar cheese

Directions

In a large skillet over medium heat, add the ground beef. Stir frequently to break the meat into crumbles as it cooks. Cook about 7-8 minutes or until the ground beef is well browned and no longer pink. Drain all the grease from the skillet. Add the tomatoes with juice, granulated sugar, salt and tomato sauce. Stir until well combined. Reduce the heat to low and simmer for 20 minutes. Remove the skillet from the heat.

While the meat sauce is simmering, cook the noodles. In a large sauce pan over medium heat, add 8 cups water. Bring the water to a boil and add the egg noodles. Boil for 6-7 minutes or until the noodles are tender. Remove the pan from the heat and drain all the water from the pasta. Add the cream cheese, sour cream and green onions to the hot noodles. Stir until the cheese softens.

Preheat the oven to 350°. Spray a 2 1/2 quart casserole dish with non stick cooking spray. Place half the noodles in the casserole dish. Spoon half the ground beef sauce over the noodles. Spread the remaining noodles over the sauce. Top the noodles with the remaining ground beef sauce. Sprinkle the cheddar cheese over the top.

Bake for 30 minutes or until the casserole is hot and bubbly. Remove from the oven and cool for 5 minutes before serving.

Taco Noodle Bake

Makes 8 servings

Ingredients

1 lb. ground beef
1/2 cup chopped onion
15 oz. can tomato sauce
1/2 cup water
1 pkg. taco seasoning mix
10 oz. pkg. egg noodles
2 cups cottage cheese
1/4 cup sour cream
1 tbs. all purpose flour
2 tsp. instant beef bouillon granules
1/4 cup chopped green onion
1 cup shredded mozzarella cheese

Directions

In a skillet over medium heat, add the ground beef and onion. Stir frequently to break the meat into crumbles as it cooks. Cook about 8 minutes or until the ground beef is well browned and no longer pink. Drain off the excess grease. Add the tomato sauce, water and taco seasoning mix. Stir until combined. Reduce the heat to low and simmer for 10 minutes. Remove the skillet from the heat.

In a large sauce pan over medium heat, add 8 cups water. Bring the water to a boil and add the egg noodles. Boil for 6-7 minutes or until the noodles are tender. Remove the pan from the heat and drain all the water from the noodles.

Add the cottage cheese, sour cream, all purpose flour, beef bouillon and green onion to the noodles. Stir until well combined. Preheat the oven to 350°. Spray a 2 1/2 quart casserole dish with non stick cooking spray. Spoon the noodles into the casserole dish. Spread the meat sauce over the noodles.

Bake for 25 minutes. Sprinkle the mozzarella cheese over the top. Bake for 5 minutes or until the dish is hot, bubbly and the cheese melted. Remove from the oven and cool for 5 minutes before serving.

Creamy Ground Beef Casserole

Makes 8 servings

Ingredients

1 1/2 lbs. ground beef
15 oz. can tomato sauce
8 oz. pkg. elbow macaroni
8 oz. pkg. cream cheese, softened
1 1/2 cups cottage cheese
1 cup sour cream
1/2 cup chopped onion
12 oz. pkg. sliced mozzarella cheese

Directions

In a skillet over medium heat, add the ground beef. Stir frequently to break the meat into crumbles as it cooks. Cook about 8 minutes or until the ground beef is well browned and no longer pink. Drain off the excess grease. Add the tomato sauce and stir until combined. Reduce the heat to low and simmer the sauce for 15 minutes. Remove the skillet from the heat.

In a large sauce pan over medium heat, add 8 cups water. Bring the water to a boil and add the macaroni. Boil for 6-7 minutes or until the macaroni is tender. Remove the pan from the heat and drain all the water from the pasta.

In a mixing bowl, add the cream cheese, cottage cheese, sour cream and onion. Stir until well combined. Preheat the oven to 350°. Spray a 9 x 13 baking dish with non stick cooking spray. Spread half the macaroni in the bottom of the baking dish. Spoon half the cream cheese sauce over the macaroni. Spoon half the ground beef sauce over the cream cheese sauce. Place half the mozzarella cheese slices over the ground beef.

Repeat the layering process one more time. Bake for 30 minutes or until the dish is hot and bubbly. Remove from the oven and cool for 5 minutes before serving.

Classic Pastitsio

Makes 8 servings

Ingredients

1 1/2 lbs. ground beef
1 cup chopped onion
15 oz. can diced tomatoes
6 oz. can tomato paste
1/4 tsp. dried thyme
1 3/4 tsp. salt
8 oz. pkg. elbow macaroni
1/2 cup crumbled feta cheese
4 egg whites, beaten
1/2 cup unsalted butter
1/3 cup all purpose flour
1/4 tsp. ground cinnamon
1 quart whole milk
4 egg yolks, beaten

Directions

In a large skillet over medium heat, add the ground beef and onion. Stir frequently to break the meat into crumbles as it cooks. Cook about 7 minutes or until the ground beef is browned and no longer pink. Drain off the excess grease.

Add the tomatoes with juice, tomato paste, thyme and 3/4 teaspoon salt. Stir frequently and bring to a boil. Place a lid on the skillet and reduce the heat to low. Stir frequently and simmer for 30 minutes. Remove the skillet from the heat.

In a large stock pot over medium heat, add 8 cups water and 1/4 teaspoon salt. Bring to a boil and add the elbow macaroni. Cook about 7 minutes or until the macaroni is tender. Remove the pan from the heat and drain all the water from the macaroni.

Add the feta cheese and egg whites to the hot pasta. Toss until combined and add to the ground beef. Toss until combined. Preheat the oven to 350°. Spray a 9 x 13 baking dish with non stick cooking spray. Spoon the filling into the baking dish.

In a sauce pan over medium heat, add the butter. When the butter melts, add the all purpose flour and cinnamon. Stir constantly and cook for 1 minute. Keep stirring and slowly add the milk. Cook until the sauce thickens and bubbles. Stir in 3/4 teaspoon salt.

Add the egg yolks to a small bowl. Add 1/4 cup sauce to the egg yolks. Whisk quickly so the egg yolks do not cook. Add the egg yolks to the sauce pan. Whisk quickly to keep the yolks from cooking. Stir constantly and cook for 1 minute. Remove the pan from the heat and pour the sauce over the beef filling in the baking dish. Do not stir. Bake for 35 minutes. Remove the dish from the oven and cool for 10 minutes before serving.

Choose A Flavor Macaroni and Cheese Casserole

While I prefer homemade macaroni and cheese, sometimes you just need to fix something from a box. This casserole is easy and even kids love it. Choose the meat to add to the casserole or leave the meat out and add vegetables if desired.

Makes 6 servings

Ingredients

1 box Velveeta shells and cheese
2 cups diced cooked chicken, ham, beef or pork
10. 75 oz. can cream of mushroom soup
4 oz. jar diced red pimentos, drained
1/4 cup chopped green bell pepper
1/4 cup chopped onion
1/2 cup whole milk
1/3 cup mayonnaise
1/2 cup shredded sharp cheddar cheese

Directions

In a large sauce pan over medium heat, add 8 cups water. Bring the water to a boil and add the macaroni from the box. Boil for 6-7 minutes or until the macaroni is tender. Remove the pan from the heat and drain all the water from the pasta.

Add the cheese sauce pouch from the box, 2 cups cooked meat, cream of mushroom soup, red pimentos, green bell pepper, onion, milk and mayonnaise to the macaroni. Stir until well combined.

Spray a 2 quart casserole dish with non stick cooking spray. Preheat the oven to 400°.

Spoon the macaroni into the prepared dish. Bake for 20 minutes. Sprinkle the cheddar cheese over the top. Bake for 5 minutes or until hot, bubbly and the cheese is melted. Remove from the oven and serve.

Overnight Pork Spaghetti Bake

Makes 8 servings

Ingredients

1 lb. ground pork
1/2 lb. ground pork sausage
1 large onion, minced
1 large green bell pepper, minced
2 garlic cloves, minced
1 tbs. vegetable oil
6 oz. can tomato paste
1 cup sliced black olives
16 oz. can cream style corn
4 oz. can sliced mushrooms, drained
1 cup shredded cheddar cheese
6 oz. spaghetti noodles, broken into 2" pieces
1 tbs. granulated sugar
1 tbs. Worcestershire sauce
1 1/2 tsp. salt
1/2 tsp. black pepper
1/4 cup grated Parmesan cheese

Directions

In a large skillet over medium heat, add the ground pork, pork sausage, onion, green bell pepper, garlic and vegetable oil. Stir frequently to break the meats into crumbles as it cooks. Cook about 10 minutes or until the pork and sausage are well browned and no longer pink. Remove the skillet from the heat and drain off the excess grease.

Spray a 12 x 8 x 2 baking dish with non stick cooking spray. Add the pork and sausage filling to the baking dish. Add the tomato paste, black olives, corn, mushrooms, cheddar cheese, spaghetti noodles, granulated sugar, Worcestershire sauce, salt and black pepper. Stir until well combined and spread the casserole in the baking dish. Sprinkle the Parmesan cheese over the top of the dish. Cover the dish with aluminum foil or a lid. Refrigerate the casserole at least 8 hours or overnight.

Remove the casserole from the refrigerator and let the casserole sit at room temperature for 1 hour. Preheat the oven to 375°. Remove the aluminum foil from the dish. Bake for 35-40 minutes or until the casserole is hot, bubbly and the noodles tender. Remove from the oven and cool for 5 minutes before serving.

Skillet Sausage Penne Casserole

Makes 6 servings

Ingredients

1 lb. penne pasta
1 lb. ground pork sausage
1 onion, chopped
1 green bell pepper, chopped
4 garlic cloves, minced
1/3 cup chicken broth
2 tbs. chili powder
2 tsp. granulated sugar
1 tsp. dried basil
1/2 tsp. black pepper
2 tbs. lime juice
2 tbs. soy sauce
14 oz. can diced tomatoes
16 oz. can tomato sauce
2 tbs. sliced black olives
1/2 cup grated Romano cheese

Directions

In a large sauce pan over medium heat, add 12 cups water. Bring the water to a boil and add the penne pasta. Boil for 6-7 minutes or until the pasta is tender. Remove the pan from the heat and drain all the water from the pasta.

In a large deep skillet, add the pork sausage, onion, green bell pepper and garlic. Stir frequently to break the meat into crumbles as it cooks. Cook about 6 minutes or until the sausage is well browned and no longer pink. Drain the grease from the skillet.

Add the chicken broth, chili powder, granulated sugar, basil, black pepper, lime juice and soy sauce to the skillet. Stir until well combined and bring to a boil. Add the tomatoes with juice, tomato sauce and pasta. Stir until well combined. Bring the casserole to a boil and simmer for 5 minutes. Remove the skillet from the heat. Sprinkle the black olives and Romano cheese over the top before serving.

Sausage Noodle Casserole

Makes 6 servings

Ingredients

8 oz. pkg. egg noodles
1 lb. ground pork sausage
10.75 oz. can cream of mushroom soup
1 cup sour cream
1/2 cup crumbled blue cheese
1 cup cooked sliced mushrooms
2 oz. jar diced red pimento, drained
2 tbs. finely chopped green bell pepper
1/2 cup soft breadcrumbs
1 tbs. unsalted butter, melted

Directions

In a large sauce pan over medium heat, add 2 quarts water. Bring the water to a boil and add the egg noodles. Boil for 6-7 minutes or until the noodles are tender. Remove the pan from the heat and drain all the water from the pasta.

In a skillet over medium heat, add the pork sausage. Stir frequently to break the meat into crumbles as it cooks. Cook about 6 minutes or until the sausage is well browned and no longer pink. Remove the skillet from the heat and drain the grease from the sausage.

Preheat the oven to 350°. Spray a 11 x 7 casserole dish with non stick cooking spray. Add the sausage, cream of mushroom soup, sour cream, blue cheese, mushrooms, red pimento and green bell pepper to the egg noodles. Toss until well combined and spoon into the prepared casserole dish.

Sprinkle the breadcrumbs over the top of the casserole and drizzle the melted butter over the breadcrumbs. Bake for 30 minutes or until hot, bubbly and the breadcrumbs are lightly browned. Remove the dish from the oven and cool for 5 minutes before serving.

Chorizo Sausage Casserole

Makes 8 servings

Ingredients

12 oz. egg noodles
1 1/2 lbs. chorizo sausage, casing removed
48 oz. jar tomato and basil spaghetti sauce
1 cup chopped fresh cilantro
4 oz. can chopped green chiles, drained
15 oz. container ricotta cheese
1 cup whipping cream
2 eggs, beaten
4 cups shredded Mexican blend cheese

Directions

In a large sauce pan over medium heat, add 12 cups water. Bring the water to a boil and add the egg noodles. Boil for 6-7 minutes or until the noodles are tender. Remove the pan from the heat and drain all the water from the noodles.

While the noodles are cooking, make the sauce. In a dutch oven over medium heat, add the chorizo sausage. Stir frequently to break the sausage into crumbles as it cooks. Cook about 8 minutes or until the chorizo is done and well browned. Drain off all the excess grease.

Add the spaghetti sauce, cilantro and green chiles to the sausage. Stir until combined and simmer the sauce for 10 minutes. Remove the pan from the heat. In a separate bowl, add the ricotta cheese, whipping cream and eggs. Stir until well combined.

Preheat the oven to 375°. Spoon 1 cup chorizo sauce in the bottom of the casserole dish. Spread 1/3 of the noodles over the sauce. Spoon 1/3 of the remaining sauce over the noodles. Spread 1/3 of the ricotta cheese mixture over the sauce. Sprinkle 1 1/3 cups Mexican blend cheese over the ricotta cheese. Repeat the layering process 2 more times.

Cover the dish with aluminum foil and bake for 45 minutes. Remove the aluminum foil from the dish and bake for 10 minutes. Remove the dish from the oven and cool for 10 minutes before serving.

Eggplant Sausage Casserole

Makes two 11 x 7 casseroles

This dish freezes well unbaked. Serve one for dinner and freeze the remaining casserole for another meal.

Ingredients

1 lb. pkg. penne pasta
2 lbs. ground Italian sausage
6 cups eggplant, peeled and cubed
1 cup chopped onion
2 garlic cloves, minced
2 tsp. paprika
28 oz. can crushed tomatoes
6 oz. can tomato paste
1 tbs. dried Italian seasoning
1 tsp. dried basil
3/4 tsp. salt
1/2 tsp. crushed red pepper flakes
15 oz. container ricotta cheese
3 cups shredded mozzarella cheese

Directions

In a large sauce pan over medium heat, add 2 quarts water. Bring the water to a boil and add the penne pasta. Boil for 6-7 minutes or until the pasta is tender. Remove the pan from the heat and drain all the water from the pasta.

In a skillet over medium heat, add the sausage. Stir frequently to break the meat into crumbles as it cooks. Cook about 8 minutes or until the sausage is well browned and no longer pink. Drain off the excess grease. Add the eggplant, onion and garlic. Stir frequently and cook for 8 minutes. Stir in the paprika and cook for 1 minute.

Add the tomatoes, tomato paste, Italian seasoning, basil, salt and red pepper flakes. Stir until combined. Reduce the heat to low and simmer for 20 minutes. Remove the skillet from the heat.

Preheat the oven to 350°. Spray two 11 x 7 casserole dishes with non stick cooking spray. In a large mixing bowl, add the ricotta cheese and 2 cups mozzarella cheese. Stir until combined. Add the penne pasta and toss until combined.

Layer 1/2 the pasta in each casserole dish. Spoon half the sauce over the noodles in each casserole dish. Sprinkle 1/2 cup mozzarella cheese over each casserole dish. Cover the dishes with aluminum foil or a lid. Bake for 30 minutes or until the casseroles are hot and bubbly. Remove the aluminum foil and cool the casseroles for 5 minutes before serving.

Pizza Pasta Bake

Makes 8 servings

Ingredients

1 lb. penne pasta
1 lb. Italian sausage, cut into 1/2" slices
1 cup chopped green bell pepper
1/2 cup chopped onion
15 oz. jar pizza sauce
1 cup sliced black olives
1 cup sliced cooked mushrooms
1/2 cup chopped fresh basil
2 cups shredded mozzarella cheese
1/2 cup sliced pepperoni
1/2 cup grated Parmesan cheese

Directions

In a large sauce pan over medium heat, add 3 quarts water. Bring the water to a boil and add the penne pasta. Boil for 6-7 minutes or until the pasta is tender. Remove the pan from the heat and drain all the water from the pasta.

In a skillet over medium heat, add the Italian sausage, green bell pepper and onion. Stir frequently to break the sausage into crumbles as it cooks. Cook about 8 minutes or until the sausage is well browned and no longer pink. Remove the skillet from the heat and drain off the excess grease.

Preheat the oven to 400°. Spray a 9 x 13 casserole dish with non stick cooking spray. Add the sausage, pizza sauce, black olives, mushrooms, basil and 1 1/2 cups mozzarella cheese to the pasta.

Toss until combined. Spoon the casserole into the prepared dish. Place the pepperoni over the top of the dish. Sprinkle the Parmesan cheese and 1/2 cup mozzarella cheese over the top.

Bake for 15 minutes or until the dish is hot, bubbly and the cheeses melted. Remove the dish from the oven and cool for 5 minutes before serving.

Pork and Noodle Bake

Makes 6 servings

Ingredients

6 oz. egg noodles
3/4 cup cottage cheese
1 cup sour cream
1/4 cup chopped green onions
1 tsp. Worcestershire sauce
1/4 tsp. plus 1/8 tsp. garlic salt
1 lb. ground pork
1 cup chopped fresh mushrooms
1/2 cup chopped green onions
1/4 cup chopped green bell pepper
2 tbs. all purpose flour
1/2 tsp. salt
1/8 tsp. ground nutmeg
1 tsp. instant chicken bouillon granules
1/4 cup water
1/2 cup shredded cheddar cheese

Directions

In a large sauce pan over medium heat, add 8 cups water. Bring the water to a boil and add the egg noodles. Boil for 6-7 minutes or until the noodles are tender. Remove the pan from the heat and drain all the water from the noodles.

In a large bowl, add the noodles, cottage cheese, 1/2 cup sour cream, green onions, Worcestershire sauce and 1/4 teaspoon garlic salt. Stir until well combined. Spoon the noodles into a 9" pie pan.

The noodles will be your crust so arrange the noodles on the bottom and up the sides of the pan to form a crust.

In a skillet over medium heat, add the ground pork and 1/8 teaspoon garlic salt. Stir frequently to break the meat into crumbles as it cooks. Cook about 8 minutes or until the pork is well browned and no longer pink. Remove the skillet from the heat and drain off all but 1 tablespoon pan drippings. Remove the pork from the skillet and set aside in a bowl.

Add the mushrooms, green onions and green bell pepper to the skillet. Place the skillet back on the stove over medium heat. Stir frequently and saute the vegetables for 5 minutes. Sprinkle the all purpose flour, salt and nutmeg over the vegetables. Stir until well combined. Add the chicken bouillon and water to the skillet. Stir constantly and cook for 4 minutes or until the sauce thickens. Add the pork back to the skillet and cook for 2 minutes. Remove the skillet from the heat and stir in 1/2 cup sour cream.

Preheat the oven to 350°. Spoon the pork filling into the pie pan over the noodle crust. Bake for 10-15 minutes or until the noodles are hot and bubbly. Sprinkle the cheddar cheese over the top of the pork. Bake for 5 minutes. Remove from the oven and cool for 5 minutes before serving.

Cheesy Pork Casserole

Makes 6 servings

Ingredients

1 1/4 lbs. ground pork
1 cup chopped fresh mushrooms
1/2 cup chopped onion
3 cups uncooked egg noodles
2 cups shredded American cheese
15 oz. can green peas, drained
10.75 oz. can cream of mushroom soup
1/4 tsp. salt
1/8 tsp. black pepper

Directions

In a skillet over medium heat, add the pork, mushrooms and onion. Stir frequently to break the meat into crumbles as it cooks. Cook about 8 minutes or until the pork is well browned and no longer pink. Remove the skillet from the heat and drain off any grease.

In a large sauce pan over medium heat, add 8 cups water. Bring the water to a boil and add the egg noodles. Boil for 6-7 minutes or until the noodles are tender. Remove the pan from the heat and drain all the water from the noodles.

Preheat the oven to 350°. Spray a 2 quart casserole dish with non stick cooking spray. Add the pork, egg noodles, 1 1/2 cups American cheese, green peas, cream of mushroom soup, salt and black pepper to the casserole dish. Stir until combined.

Cover the dish with aluminum foil or a lid. Bake for 30 minutes or until the casserole is hot and bubbly. Remove the aluminum foil from the dish. Sprinkle 1/2 cup American cheese over the top of the casserole. Bake for 5 minutes. Remove the dish from the oven and cool for 5 minutes before serving.

Pork Noodle Skillet

Makes 4 servings

Ingredients

2 tbs. vegetable oil
1 1/2 lbs. boneless pork loin, cut into bite size pieces
1 cup sliced carrot
1 cup thinly sliced celery
1/3 cup chopped onion
16 oz. can tomato sauce
2 cups water
1/3 cup ketchup
1/2 cup sliced fresh mushrooms
1/2 tsp. salt
1/4 tsp. garlic powder
1/4 tsp. dried basil
1/4 tsp. black pepper
4 oz. uncooked egg noodles

Directions

In a skillet over medium heat, add 1 tablespoon vegetable oil and the pork. Stir frequently and cook about 5 minutes or until the pork is browned on all sides. Remove the pork from the skillet and set aside for now.

Add 1 tablespoon vegetable oil to the skillet. Add the carrot, celery and onion. Saute the vegetables for 5 minutes. Add the tomato sauce, water, ketchup, mushrooms, salt, garlic powder, basil and black pepper. Stir until well combined and the sauce comes to a boil. Add the egg noodles and pork to the skillet. Stir until combined and place a lid on the skillet. Simmer for 30 minutes or until the pork and noodles are tender. Remove the skillet from the heat and serve.

Italian Sausage Lasagna Casserole

Makes 6 servings

Ingredients

1 lb. ground Italian sausage
1 onion, chopped
1 garlic clove, minced
3 tbs. dried parsley flakes
16 oz. can diced tomatoes
15 oz. can tomato sauce
1 tsp. granulated sugar
1 tsp. dried basil
1/2 tsp. salt
10 oz. penne pasta
16 oz. container ricotta cheese
1/4 cup plus 2 tbs. grated Parmesan cheese
2 cups shredded mozzarella cheese
1 1/2 tsp. dried oregano

Directions

In a skillet over medium heat, add the Italian sausage, onion and garlic. Stir frequently to break the meat into crumbles as it cooks. Cook about 8 minutes or until the sausage is well browned and no longer pink. Drain all the grease from the skillet.

Add the parsley, tomatoes with juice, tomato sauce, granulated sugar, basil and salt to the skillet. Bring the sauce to a boil and reduce the heat to low. Stir frequently and simmer for 40 minutes. Remove the skillet from the heat.

In a large sauce pan over medium heat, add 2 quarts water. Bring the water to a boil and add the penne pasta. Boil for 6-7 minutes or until the pasta is tender. Remove the pan from the heat and drain all the water from the pasta.

Preheat the oven to 350°. Spray a 9 x 13 casserole dish with non stick cooking spray. In a large bowl, add the ricotta cheese, 1/4 cup Parmesan cheese, 1 cup mozzarella cheese and oregano. Stir until well combined. Add the pasta and toss until well blended. Spread the pasta into the prepared casserole dish. Spoon the sauce over the pasta.

Sprinkle 1 cup mozzarella cheese and 2 tablespoons Parmesan cheese over the top. Cover the dish with aluminum foil or a lid. Bake for 45 minutes. Remove the aluminum foil from the dish. Bake for 5 minutes. Remove the dish from the oven and cool for 5 minutes before serving.

Ham Noodle Skillet

Makes 4 servings

Ingredients

4 oz. jar whole mushrooms
2 cups cubed cooked ham
1/4 cup chopped green bell pepper
1/4 cup chopped onion
2 tbs. unsalted butter, melted
1/8 tsp. black pepper
Pinch of paprika
1 tsp. Worcestershire sauce
1 cup water
4 oz. dry egg noodles
1 cup sour cream

Directions

Drain the mushrooms but reserve 1/4 cup liquid. In a large skillet over medium heat, add the ham, green bell pepper, onion and butter. Saute for 4 minutes. Add the black pepper, paprika, Worcestershire sauce, water, egg noodles and 1/4 cup reserved mushroom liquid. Stir until combined and bring to a boil.

Place a lid on the skillet and reduce the heat to low. Simmer for 15 minutes or until the noodles are tender. Add the mushrooms and cook for 5 minutes. Remove the skillet from the heat and stir in the sour cream.

Ham Cheddar Casserole

Makes 4 servings

Ingredients

1 1/4 cups elbow macaroni
3/4 tsp. salt
2 tbs. unsalted butter
2 tbs. all purpose flour
1/4 tsp. dry mustard
1 cup whole milk
1 cup diced fully cooked ham
1 1/2 cups shredded cheddar cheese
Black pepper to taste

Directions

In a large sauce pan over medium heat, add 8 cups water and 1/2 teaspoon salt. Bring the water to a boil and add the macaroni. Boil for 6-7 minutes or until the macaroni is tender. Remove the pan from the heat and drain all the water from the macaroni.

In a sauce pan over medium heat, add the butter. When the butter melts, add the all purpose flour, dry mustard and 1/4 teaspoon salt. Stir until well combined and cook for 1 minute. Slowly add the milk and cook until the sauce thickens and bubbles. Stir constantly once you add the milk. Remove the pan from the heat and stir in the ham and 1 cup cheddar cheese. Remove the pan from the heat.

Preheat the oven to 350°. Spray a 2 quart casserole dish with non stick cooking spray. Add the macaroni to the casserole dish. Pour the cheese sauce over the macaroni and stir until combined. Season to taste with black pepper. Bake for 20 minutes or until the casserole is hot and bubbly. Sprinkle 1/2 cup cheddar cheese over the top and bake for 5 minutes. Remove the dish from the oven and serve.

Spaghetti Ham Casserole

Makes 6 servings

Ingredients

6 oz. pkg. spaghetti noodles
4 garlic cloves, minced
2 1/2 tbs. olive oil
1/4 cup all purpose flour
1/4 tsp. salt
1/8 tsp. black pepper
3/4 cup half and half
1 1/2 cups whole milk
1/2 cup chopped cooked ham
1/4 cup grated Parmesan cheese

Directions

In a large sauce pan over medium heat, add 8 cups water. Bring the water to a boil and add the spaghetti. Boil for 6-7 minutes or until the spaghetti noodles are tender. Remove the pan from the heat and drain all the water from the noodles.

In a skillet over medium heat, add the garlic and olive oil. Saute the garlic for 4 minutes. Add the all purpose flour, salt and black pepper. Stir constantly and cook for 2 minutes. Keep stirring and slowly add the half and half and whole milk. Stir constantly until the sauce thickens and bubbles.

Add the spaghetti noodles and ham to the skillet. Stir until combined and remove the skillet from the heat. Preheat the oven to 350°. Spray a 2 quart casserole dish with non stick cooking spray. Spoon the casserole into the dish.

Cover the casserole with aluminum foil or a lid. Bake for 20 minutes. Remove the aluminum foil and sprinkle the Parmesan cheese over the top. Bake for 10 minutes or until the cheese is melted, lightly browned and the casserole hot. Remove the dish from the oven and serve.

Creamy Ham Medley

Makes 4 servings

Ingredients

1/2 cup chopped onion
1/4 cup thinly sliced celery
1/4 cup chopped green bell pepper
2 tbs. unsalted butter
2 tbs. all purpose flour
1 cup whole milk
1 cup cottage cheese
1 cup cubed cooked ham
2 cups cooked egg noodles
1/2 tsp. salt
1/8 tsp. black pepper

Directions

In a skillet over medium heat, add the onion, celery, green bell pepper and butter. Saute the vegetables for 5 minutes. Sprinkle the flour over the vegetables and stir until combined. Stir constantly and cook for 1 minute. Add the milk and cottage cheese. Stir constantly and cook until the sauce thickens and bubbles.

Remove the skillet from the heat and stir in the ham, noodles, salt and black pepper. Preheat the oven to 350°. Spray a 1 quart casserole dish with non stick cooking spray. Add the casserole to the dish. Bake for 25 minutes or until the casserole is hot and bubbly. Remove from the oven and serve.

Chicken Ham Noodle Casserole

Makes 6 servings

Ingredients

8 oz. pkg. egg noodles
1 1/2 cups chopped cooked ham
1 cup shredded cheddar cheese
10.75 oz. can cream of chicken soup
1/2 cup whole milk
2 tbs. unsalted butter

Directions

In a large sauce pan over medium heat, add 10 cups water. Bring the water to a boil and add the egg noodles. Boil for 8 minutes or until the noodles are tender. Remove the pan from the heat and drain all the water from the noodles.

Preheat the oven to 375°. Spray a 2 quart casserole dish with non stick cooking spray. Place half the egg noodles in the bottom of the casserole dish. Sprinkle 3/4 cup ham and 3/4 cup cheddar cheese over the noodles.

In a small bowl, add the cream of chicken soup and milk. Stir until combined and pour half the soup over the ham and cheese. Repeat the layering process one more time using the remaining noodles, 3/4 cup ham and 1/4 cup cheddar cheese. Cut the butter into small pieces and place over the top of the casserole.

Bake for 30 minutes or until the casserole is hot, bubbly and the cheese melted. Remove the dish from the oven and serve.

Cream Cheese Ham Casserole

Makes 8 servings

Ingredients

8 oz. egg noodles
10.75 oz. can cream of mushroom soup
8 oz. container chive and onion cream cheese
2/3 cup whole milk
2 cups chopped cooked ham
1 1/2 cups chopped fresh broccoli
10 oz. pkg. frozen asparagus, thawed
1 cup thinly sliced carrots
2 cups shredded mozzarella cheese
1 cup shredded cheddar cheese
1/2 cup crushed garlic croutons

Directions

In a large sauce pan over medium heat, add 10 cups water. Bring the water to a boil and add the egg noodles. Boil for 6-7 minutes or until the noodles are tender. Remove the pan from the heat and drain all the water from the noodles.

Preheat the oven to 400°. Spray a 9 x 13 baking dish with non stick cooking spray. Add the cream of mushroom soup, cream cheese, milk, ham, broccoli, asparagus, carrots and mozzarella cheese to the egg noodles. Stir until combined.

Spread the filling into the prepared casserole dish. Sprinkle the cheddar cheese over the top. Sprinkle the crushed croutons over the cheese. Bake for 30 minutes or until the casserole is hot, bubbly and the cheeses melted. Remove the dish from the oven and cool for 5 minutes before serving.

Creamy Ham & Chicken Lasagna Bake

Makes 8 servings

Ingredients

10 oz. pkg. rigatoni pasta
1/3 cup plus 2 tbs. unsalted butter
2 cups fresh sliced mushrooms
2 cups chopped cooked chicken
2 cups chopped cooked ham
1/3 cup all purpose flour
3 cups whole milk
1 1/2 cups freshly grated Parmesan cheese
1/2 cup whipping cream
3/4 tsp. dried basil
1/2 tsp. salt
1/4 tsp. black pepper

Directions

In a large sauce pan over medium heat, add 2 quarts water. Bring the water to a boil and add the rigatoni pasta. Boil for 6-7 minutes or until the rigatoni is tender. Remove the pan from the heat and drain all the water from the pasta.

In a skillet, add 2 tablespoons butter and the mushrooms. Saute for 5 minutes. Remove the skillet from the heat and spoon the butter and mushrooms into a mixing bowl. Add the chicken and ham to the mixing bowl. Toss until blended.

Add 1/3 cup butter to the skillet used to cook the mushrooms. Place the skillet over medium heat. When the butter melts, add the all purpose flour. Stir constantly and cook for 1 minute. Keep stirring and add the whole milk. Cook until the sauce thickens and bubbles. Remove the skillet from the heat and add the Parmesan cheese, whipping cream, basil, salt and black pepper. Stir until well combined and the cheese melts. Pour the sauce over the chicken and ham in the bowl. Stir until combined.

Preheat the oven to 350°. Spray a 9 x 13 casserole dish with non stick cooking spray. Add the noodles and chicken and ham filling to the casserole dish. Toss until combined. Cover the dish with aluminum foil or a lid. Bake for 30 minutes or until hot and bubbly. Remove the dish from the oven and serve.

Sesame Chicken Noodle Bake

Makes 4 servings

Ingredients

4 boneless skinless chicken breast, 4 oz. each
1/4 cup light brown sugar
1/3 cup soy sauce
1/4 cup dry sherry
2 tbs. white wine vinegar
2 tbs. sesame oil
1 tsp. minced fresh ginger
1 garlic clove, minced
1/4 tsp. black pepper
1/4 tsp. cayenne pepper
2 tsp. cornstarch
1 red bell pepper, cut into thin strips
1/4 cup sliced green onions
1 cup shredded red cabbage
1/2 cup chopped walnuts
2 tbs. sesame seeds
2 tbs. minced fresh parsley
8 oz. cooked egg noodles

Directions

Cut the chicken breast into thin strips and place the chicken in a bowl. In a small bowl, add the brown sugar, soy sauce, sherry, white wine vinegar, sesame oil, ginger, garlic, black pepper and cayenne pepper. Stir until well combined. Reserve 1/4 cup marinade in a separate bowl. Pour the remaining marinade over the chicken. Toss until the chicken is coated in the marinade. Cover the bowl and chill for 30 minutes.

Remove the chicken from the refrigerator and drain off the marinade. Add the chicken, 1/4 cup reserved marinade and cornstarch to a large oven proof skillet over medium heat. Stir frequently and cook for 6 minutes or until the chicken is tender and no longer pink. Remove the skillet from the heat.

Preheat the oven to 350°. Add the red bell pepper, green onions, cabbage, walnuts, sesame seeds and parsley to the skillet. Stir until combined. Add the cooked egg noodles and toss until combined. Bake for 10 minutes or until the noodles are hot. Remove the skillet from the oven and serve.

Chicken Asparagus Pasta Supper

Makes 8 servings

Ingredients

4 tbs. vegetable oil
1 1/2 lbs. fresh asparagus, cut into 2" pieces
2 cups sliced fresh mushrooms
1 1/2 cups chopped broccoli florets
2 carrots, julienned
2 zucchini, thinly sliced
3 green onions, sliced
1/2 tsp. salt
4 skinless boneless chicken breast, cubed
1/2 cup frozen green peas
2 tbs. unsalted butter
2 tbs. all purpose flour
1/4 tsp. black pepper
2 cups whole milk
1 chicken bouillon cube
8 oz. vermicelli noodles, cooked

Directions

In a large skillet over medium heat, add 2 tablespoons vegetable oil, asparagus, mushrooms, broccoli, carrots, zucchini, green onions and salt. Saute the vegetables for 5 minutes. Remove the vegetables from the skillet and set aside for the moment.

Add 2 tablespoons vegetable oil to the skillet. Add the chicken and cook for 6-7 minutes or until the chicken is browned and no longer pink. Add the vegetables back to the skillet along with the green peas. Stir until combined. Cook for 5 minutes or until the vegetables are crisp tender. Remove the skillet from the heat.

In a sauce pan over medium heat, add the butter. When the butter melts, add the all purpose flour. Stir constantly and cook for 2 minutes. Add the black pepper, milk and chicken bouillon cube. Stir constantly and cook until the sauce thickens and bubbles. Remove the pan from the heat and add to the chicken and vegetables in the skillet. Add the vermicelli noodles to the skillet. Toss until well combined and serve.

Cheesy Chicken Enchilada Skillet

Makes 6 servings

Ingredients

8 oz. small pasta shells
14 oz. can fire roasted diced tomatoes
10 oz. can enchilada sauce
2 cups water
8 green onions, sliced
2 tsp. chili powder
15 oz. can black beans, drained
1 1/2 cups whole kernel corn
2 cups cooked chicken
2 cups shredded sharp cheddar cheese

Directions

In a large skillet over medium heat, add the pasta shells, tomatoes, enchilada sauce, water, 1/2 the green onions and chili powder. Stir until combined and bring to a boil. When the pasta boils, reduce the heat to low. Simmer for 10-12 minutes or until the pasta is tender. Stir the pasta frequently while cooking to prevent sticking.

Add the black beans, corn, chicken and cheddar cheese. Stir until combined and cook until thoroughly heated. Remove the skillet from the heat and sprinkle the remaining green onions over the top before serving.

Chicken Pasta Broccoli Bake

Makes 8 servings

Ingredients

1/2 cup plus 3 tbs. unsalted butter
1/2 cup chopped onion
1/2 cup chopped red bell pepper
2 garlic cloves, minced
1/4 cup all purpose flour
3 1/2 cups chicken broth
1 1/2 cups half and half
1 cup shredded Parmesan cheese
1/4 tsp. salt
1/4 tsp. cayenne pepper
20 oz. pkg. refrigerated spinach tortellini
4 cups chopped fresh broccoli
4 cups cooked chopped chicken
1/2 cup grated Parmesan cheese
1 cup butter cracker crumbs
1/2 cup chopped pecans

Directions

In a large skillet over medium heat, add 1/2 cup butter, onion, red bell pepper and garlic. Saute the vegetables for 5 minutes. Sprinkle the all purpose flour over the vegetables. Stir constantly and cook for 1 minute. Add the chicken broth and the half and half. Stir constantly and cook until the sauce slightly thickens and bubbles. Remove the skillet from the heat and add 1 cup shredded Parmesan cheese, salt and cayenne pepper. Stir until combined and the Parmesan cheese melts.

Add the spinach tortellini, broccoli and chicken to the skillet. Stir until combined. Preheat the oven to 350°. Spray a 9 x 13 casserole dish with non stick cooking spray. Add the tortellini filling to the casserole dish.

In a small bowl, add 3 tablespoons butter, 1/2 cup grated Parmesan cheese, cracker crumbs and pecans. Using a fork, cut the butter into the dry ingredients until combined and you have crumbles. Sprinkle the crumbles over the top of the casserole. Bake for 45 minutes or until the casserole is hot and bubbly. Remove the dish from the oven and serve.

Chicken Linguine Casserole

Makes 8 servings

Ingredients

1 lb. boneless skinless chicken breast, cut into bite size pieces
2 tbs. unsalted butter
1/2 cup dry sherry
1/2 cup water
1 onion, diced
2 cups sliced fresh mushrooms
8 oz. linguine noodles
2/3 cup all purpose flour
2 cups chicken broth
1 cup sour cream
1/2 tsp. black pepper
1 cup shredded Monterey Jack cheese
1/2 cup freshly grated Parmesan cheese
1/2 cup seasoned breadcrumbs

Directions

Add the chicken and butter to a large skillet over medium heat. Cook for 5 minutes or until the chicken is almost done. Add the sherry, water, onion and mushrooms. Stir until combined and saute about 5 minutes or until the chicken and vegetables are tender.

While the chicken is cooking, cook the linguine noodles. In a large sauce pan over medium heat, add 10 cups water. Bring the water to a boil and add the linguine noodles. Boil for 6-7 minutes or until the noodles are tender. Remove the pan from the heat and drain all the water from the noodles.

Sprinkle the all purpose flour over the chicken and vegetables. Stir until well combined. Add the chicken broth to the skillet. Stir occasionally and simmer about 8 minutes or until the sauce thickens. Remove the skillet from the heat and add to the linguine noodles. Add the sour cream, black pepper and Monterey Jack cheese to the noodles. Stir until well combined.

Preheat the oven to 350°. Spray a 9 x 13 casserole dish with non stick cooking spray. Spoon the noodles into the casserole dish. Sprinkle the Parmesan cheese over the top. Sprinkle the seasoned breadcrumbs over the top. Cover the dish with aluminum foil. Bake for 30 minutes or until the casserole is hot and bubbly. Remove the aluminum foil and bake for 10 minutes. Remove the dish from the oven and cool for 5 minutes before serving.

Chicken, Tomato & Sausage Skillet

Makes 4 servings

Ingredients

7 oz. pkg. spaghetti noodles
1 onion, chopped
1 green bell pepper, chopped
2 garlic cloves, minced
1/4 lb. ground pork sausage
1 lb. boneless skinless chicken breast, cut into bite size pieces
1/4 cup water
29 oz. can diced tomatoes, drained
3 tbs. tomato paste
2 tsp. dried basil
1 chicken bouillon cube
1/2 tsp. black pepper
Grated Parmesan cheese, optional

Directions

In a large sauce pan over medium heat, add 8 cups water. Bring the water to a boil and add the spaghetti noodles. Boil for 6-7 minutes or until the noodles are tender. Remove the pan from the heat and drain all the water from the noodles.

In a large skillet over medium heat, add the onion, green bell pepper, garlic and pork sausage. Stir frequently to break the sausage into crumbles as it cooks. Cook for 5 minutes. Add the chicken to the skillet. Stir frequently and cook for 6 minutes or until the chicken is no longer pink. Drain the excess grease from the skillet.

Add 1/4 cup water, tomatoes, tomato paste, basil, chicken bouillon cube and black pepper to the skillet. Stir until well combined and bring to a boil. Add the spaghetti and toss until combined. Simmer for 3 minutes or until the dish is hot and bubbly. Remove the skillet from the heat and serve. Sprinkle with Parmesan cheese if desired.

Chicken Macaroni Bake

Makes 6 servings

Ingredients

1 cup elbow macaroni
1 cup shredded cheddar cheese
1 onion, chopped
1 green bell pepper, chopped
10.75 oz. can cream of mushroom soup
2 oz. jar diced red pimento
1/2 cup mayonnaise
1/3 cup whole milk
2 cups chopped cooked chicken
1/2 cup Italian seasoned breadcrumbs

Directions

In a large sauce pan over medium heat, add 8 cups water. Bring the water to a boil and add the macaroni. Boil for 6-7 minutes or until the macaroni is tender. Remove the pan from the heat and drain all the water from the macaroni.

Preheat the oven to 350°. Spray a 11 x 7 casserole dish with non stick cooking spray. Add the cheddar cheese, onion, green bell pepper, cream of mushroom soup, red pimento, mayonnaise, milk and chicken to the macaroni. Toss until well combined.

Spoon the filling into the prepared casserole dish. Sprinkle the breadcrumbs over the top of the casserole. Bake for 30 minutes or until the casserole is hot, bubbly and the breadcrumbs golden brown. Remove from the oven and serve.

Spinach Chicken Noodle Bake

Makes 8 servings

Ingredients

6 oz. penne pasta
10 oz. pkg. frozen spinach, thawed
2 cups cooked chopped chicken
2 cups shredded cheddar cheese
1/3 cup finely chopped onion
1/4 tsp. ground nutmeg
1 tbs. cornstarch
1/2 tsp. salt
1/4 tsp. black pepper
1 tbs. soy sauce
10.75 oz. can cream of mushroom soup
1 cup sour cream
4 oz. jar sliced mushrooms, drained
1/3 cup mayonnaise
1 cup freshly grated Parmesan cheese
2 tbs. melted unsalted butter
1 cup chopped pecans

Directions

In a large sauce pan over medium heat, add 2 quarts water. Bring the water to a boil and add the penne pasta. Boil for 6-7 minutes or until the pasta is tender. Remove the pan from the heat and drain all the water from the pasta.

You need to remove all the moisture from the spinach. Press the spinach with paper towels if needed to remove the moisture. In a mixing bowl, add the spinach, chicken, cheddar cheese, onion, nutmeg, cornstarch, salt, black pepper, soy sauce, cream of mushroom soup, sour cream, mushrooms and mayonnaise. Stir until well combined. Add the penne pasta and toss until combined.

Preheat the oven to 350°. Spoon the filling into a 9 x 13 casserole dish. Sprinkle the Parmesan cheese over the top of the casserole. In a small sauce pan over medium heat, add the butter and pecans. Stir constantly and cook for 4 minutes or until the pecans are toasted. Remove the pan from the heat and spoon over the top of the casserole.

Cover the dish with aluminum foil or a lid. Bake for 45-50 minutes or until the casserole is hot and bubbly. Remove the dish from the oven and cool for 5 minutes before serving.

Smoked Sausage Noodle Bake

Makes 4 servings

Ingredients

1 1/2 cups diced smoked sausage
3 tbs. finely chopped onion
1 1/2 cups cooked green peas
10.75 oz. can cream of chicken soup
8 oz. pkg. egg noodles, cooked
1/4 tsp. salt
3/4 cup whole milk
1 cup herb croutons, crushed
3 tbs. unsalted butter, melted

Directions

Preheat the oven to 350°. Spray a 2 quart casserole dish with non stick cooking spray. Add the smoked sausage, onion, green peas, cream of chicken soup, egg noodles, salt and whole milk to the casserole dish. Stir until combined.

Sprinkle the croutons over the top. Drizzle the melted butter over the croutons. Bake for 30-40 minutes or until the top is golden brown and the casserole hot and bubbly. Remove the dish from the oven and serve.

Smoked Sausage Vegetable Pasta Skillet

Makes 6 servings

Ingredients

5 oz. pkg. egg noodles
3 cups sliced fresh mushrooms
1 cup fresh broccoli florets
1/2 cup chopped zucchini
1/4 cup chopped onion
1/4 cup chopped green bell pepper
1 tsp. dried oregano
1/4 tsp. garlic powder
3 tbs. unsalted butter
1 lb. smoked sausage, cut into 1/2" slices
1/2 cup grated Parmesan cheese
6 cherry tomatoes, halved

Directions

In a large sauce pan over medium heat, add 8 cups water. Bring the water to a boil and add the egg noodles. Boil for 6-7 minutes or until the noodles are tender. Remove the pan from the heat and drain all the water from the noodles.

In a large deep skillet over medium heat, add the mushrooms, broccoli, zucchini, onion, green bell pepper, oregano, garlic powder and butter. Saute the vegetables for 5 minutes. Add the smoked sausage and cook for 3 minutes.

Add the egg noodles and 1/4 cup grated Parmesan cheese to the skillet. Stir until well blended and cook until thoroughly heated. Remove the skillet from the heat and sprinkle 1/4 cup Parmesan cheese and the cherry tomatoes over the top before serving.

Smoked Sausage Broccoli Skillet

Makes 4 servings

Ingredients

1 lb. fresh broccoli florets
9 oz. pkg. refrigerated fettuccine
3 eggs
3/4 cup whipping cream
3/4 tsp. black pepper
2 tbs. unsalted butter
1 cup sliced fresh mushrooms
1 garlic clove, minced
1 lb. smoked sausage, sliced
1 cup grated Parmesan cheese

Directions

In a dutch oven over medium heat, add 12 cups water. Bring the water to a boil and add the broccoli and fettuccine. Boil for 4 minutes or until the broccoli is tender. Remove the pan from the heat and drain all the water from the broccoli and fettuccine. Rinse the pasta and broccoli with cold water and drain all the water again.

In a large bowl, add the eggs, whipping cream and black pepper. Whisk until well combined. Add the fettuccine and broccoli to the bowl. Toss until combined.

Add the butter, mushrooms and garlic to a large skillet. Saute the vegetables for 5 minutes. Add the smoked sausage and cook for 5 minutes or until the smoked sausage is lightly browned. Add the fettuccine to the skillet. Stir gently and cook for 5 minutes or until the sauce thickens and is well combined. Remove the skillet from the heat and sprinkle the Parmesan cheese over the hot pasta.

Banquet Stroganoff

I take this dish to potlucks at church all the time. You will come home with an empty dish.

Makes 8 servings

Ingredients

1/2 cup unsalted butter
2 lbs. fresh shrimp, peeled and deveined
2 cups cooked chopped chicken
8 oz. smoked sausage, cut into 1/2" slices
2 cups sliced fresh mushrooms
1/2 cup onion, chopped
1 garlic clove, minced
1/4 cup all purpose flour
1 cup chicken broth
1/2 cup whole milk
1/2 cup white wine
1 tsp. ketchup
1/2 tsp. Worcestershire sauce
8 oz. container sour cream
3 cups cooked elbow macaroni
1 tbs. chopped fresh dill

Directions

In a dutch oven, add 1/4 cup butter and the shrimp. Saute for 3 minutes or until the shrimp just begin to turn pink. Remove the shrimp from the dutch oven and place in a large bowl. Add the chicken and smoked sausage to the dutch oven. Cook about 5 minutes or until the chicken and sausage are well browned. Remove the chicken and sausage from the dutch oven and add to the bowl with the shrimp.

Add 1/4 cup butter, mushrooms, onion and garlic to the dutch oven. Saute the vegetables for 5 minutes. Sprinkle the all purpose flour over the vegetables. Stir constantly and cook for 2 minutes. Add the chicken broth, milk, white wine, ketchup and Worcestershire sauce. Stir constantly and cook until the sauce thickens and bubbles. Add the sour cream, shrimp, chicken, smoked sausage and macaroni to the dutch oven. Stir only until combined. Remove the pan from the heat.

Preheat the oven to 350°. Spray a 9 x 13 casserole dish with non stick cooking spray. Spoon the filling into the casserole dish. Sprinkle the fresh dill over the top. Bake for 25 minutes or until the dish is hot and the shrimp fully cooked. Remove the dish from the oven and serve.

Frankaroni Potluck Casserole

This casserole is loved by kids and adults. I always make this for the children at church.

Makes 6 servings

Ingredients

8 oz. pkg. elbow macaroni
1/2 cup unsalted butter
1 cup chopped onion
1 cup thinly sliced celery
2 tbs. all purpose flour
2 1/2 cups whole milk
1 lb. hot dogs, cut into bite size pieces
2 cups shredded cheddar cheese
1 tbs. yellow prepared mustard
1/2 tsp. salt
1/8 tsp. black pepper

Directions

In a large sauce pan over medium heat, add 10 cups water. Bring the water to a boil and add the macaroni. Boil for 6-7 minutes or until the macaroni is tender. Remove the pan from the heat and drain all the water from the pasta.

In sauce pan over low heat, add the butter, onion and celery. Saute for 6 minutes or until the vegetables are tender. Increase the heat to medium and stir in the all purpose flour. Cook for 2 minutes. Slowly add the milk and stir until the sauce thickens and bubbles.

Add the hot dogs, 1 1/2 cups cheddar cheese, mustard, salt and black pepper. Stir constantly until the cheese melts. Remove the sauce pan from the heat.

Preheat the oven to 350°. Spray a 2 1/2 quart casserole dish with non stick cooking spray. Add the noodles to the casserole dish. Pour the sauce over the noodles and toss until combined. Bake for 30 minutes or until the casserole is hot and bubbly. Sprinkle the remaining 1/2 cup cheddar cheese over the top. Bake for 5 minutes. Remove the dish from the oven and cool for 5 minutes before serving.

Bacon Spaghetti

Makes 4 servings

Ingredients

10 slices bacon, chopped
1/2 cup chopped onion
1/2 cup chopped green bell pepper
8 oz. dry spaghetti noodles, broken into pieces
2 cups boiling water
29 oz. can diced tomatoes
2 tbs. Worcestershire sauce
4 tbs. grated Parmesan cheese

Directions

In a large skillet over medium heat, add the bacon, onion and green bell pepper. Saute for 5-7 minutes or until the bacon is done and crispy. Drain off the excess grease.

Add the spaghetti noodles, water, tomatoes with juice and Worcestershire sauce. Stir until well combined. Place a lid on the skillet and reduce the heat to low. Stir occasionally and simmer for 20 minutes. Remove the skillet from the heat and sprinkle the Parmesan cheese over the top before serving.

Cabbage Bacon Noodle Casserole

Makes 6 servings

Ingredients

6 tbs. unsalted butter
4 cups chopped green cabbage
1 onion, chopped
1/4 tsp. salt
1/4 tsp. black pepper
1 tbs. all purpose flour
2 cups half and half cream
1 cup crumbled cooked bacon
8 oz. fettuccine noodles, cooked
1 cup shredded Parmesan cheese

Directions

In a dutch oven over medium heat, add the butter, cabbage, onion, salt and black pepper. Stir constantly and cook for 10 minutes. Sprinkle the all purpose flour over the cabbage. Stir constantly and add the half and half. Continue stirring until the sauce is smooth and thickens. Remove the pan from the heat.

Preheat the oven to 350°. Spray a 2 quart casserole dish with non stick cooking spray. Add the bacon, noodles, 1/2 cup Parmesan cheese and the cabbage to the dish. Stir until well combined. Sprinkle 1/2 cup Parmesan cheese over the top of the casserole. Bake for 20 minutes or until the dish is bubbly and the cheese melts. Remove the dish from the oven and serve.

Gorgonzola Bacon Mac & Cheese Bake

Makes 6 servings

Ingredients

8 oz. elbow macaroni
1 cup whole milk
3/4 cup shredded Gorgonzola cheese
1 cup sour cream
1/2 tsp. black pepper
1 cup crumbled cooked bacon
1/2 cup dry breadcrumbs
2 tbs. melted unsalted butter

Directions

In a large sauce pan over medium heat, add 2 quarts water. Bring the water to a boil and add the elbow macaroni. Boil for 6-7 minutes or until the macaroni is tender. Remove the pan from the heat and drain all the water from the macaroni.

In a small sauce pan over medium heat, add the milk and Gorgonzola cheese. Stir constantly until the cheese melts. Remove the pan from the heat and stir in the sour cream, black pepper and bacon.

Preheat the oven to 350°. Spray a 1 1/2 quart casserole dish with non stick cooking spray. Add the macaroni and cheese sauce to the dish. Stir until combined. Sprinkle the breadcrumbs over the top of the casserole. Drizzle the melted butter over the breadcrumbs.

Bake for 30 minutes or until hot, bubbly and the breadcrumbs golden brown. Remove the dish from the oven and cool for 5 minutes before serving.

Parmesan Turkey Broccoli Casserole

Makes a 9" square baking pan

Ingredients

6 oz. angel hair pasta
4 eggs, beaten
3 tbs. melted unsalted butter
2/3 cup plus 1/4 cup grated Parmesan cheese
2 cups broccoli florets
2 garlic cloves, minced
1 red bell pepper, thinly sliced
2 tsp. dried basil
1 1/2 cups diced cooked turkey
1/2 cup whole milk
1/4 tsp. salt
1/4 tsp. black pepper

Directions

Break the pasta into sections. In a large sauce pan over medium heat, add 8 cups water. Bring the water to a boil and add the pasta. Boil for 6-7 minutes or until the pasta is tender. Remove the pan from the heat and drain all the water from the pasta.

Preheat the oven to 350°. Add 2 beaten eggs, 2 tablespoons melted butter and 1/3 cup Parmesan cheese to the pasta. Stir until well combined. Spray a 9" square baking dish with non stick cooking spray. Spread the noodles into the baking dish. The noodles will be the crust so push the noodles up the sides of the pan. Bake the noodles for 10 minutes.

Add the broccoli to a large sauce pan over medium heat. Add water to cover the broccoli. Cook for 8 minutes or until the broccoli is tender. Remove the pan from the heat and drain all the water from the pan. Add 1 tablespoon melted butter to the broccoli. Place the pan back over medium heat. Add the garlic, red bell pepper and basil to the pan. Saute the garlic and broccoli for 3 minutes or until the garlic is tender. Add the turkey and 1/3 cup Parmesan cheese. Stir until combined.

In a small bowl, add 2 beaten eggs, milk, salt, black pepper and 1/4 cup Parmesan cheese. Whisk until well combined and add to the broccoli. Stir until combined and remove the pan from the heat. Spoon the broccoli turkey filling into the casserole dish. Place aluminum foil or a lid over the top of the casserole dish. Bake for 30 minutes or until hot and bubbly. Remove from the oven and cool for 10 minutes before removing the aluminum foil. Remove the aluminum foil and serve.

Turkey Tomato Casserole

Makes 6 servings

Ingredients

2 cups elbow macaroni
2 cups chopped cooked turkey
28 oz. can Italian seasoned diced tomatoes
10 oz. pkg. frozen spinach, thawed and drained
1/4 cup chopped onion
2 garlic cloves, minced
1/2 cup freshly grated Parmesan cheese
1 cup shredded mozzarella cheese
1/2 cup seasoned breadcrumbs
2 tbs. unsalted butter, melted

Directions

In a large sauce pan over medium heat, add 2 quarts water. Bring the water to a boil and add the elbow macaroni. Boil for 6-7 minutes or until the macaroni is tender. Remove the pan from the heat and drain all the water from the macaroni.

Preheat the oven to 350°. Spray a 11 x 7 casserole dish with non stick cooking spray. Add the turkey, tomatoes with juice, spinach, onion, garlic and Parmesan cheese to the noodles. Stir until combined. Spoon the filling into the casserole dish.

Sprinkle the mozzarella cheese over the top of the casserole dish. Sprinkle the breadcrumbs over the top of the cheese. Drizzle the melted butter over the top of the breadcrumbs. Cover the dish with aluminum foil or a lid. Bake for 45 minutes. Remove the aluminum foil and bake for 10 minutes. Remove the dish from the oven and serve.

Ham and Turkey Spaghetti Casserole

Makes 8 servings

Ingredients

8 oz. pkg. spaghetti noodles
2 tbs. unsalted butter
6 green onions, sliced
1 1/2 cups sliced fresh mushrooms
1 1/2 cups chopped cooked ham
1 1/2 cups chopped cooked turkey
12 oz. carton cottage cheese
1 cup sour cream
2 tbs. whole milk
1/4 tsp. salt
1/4 tsp. celery salt
1/2 tsp. black pepper
1 cup shredded sharp cheddar cheese

Directions

In a large sauce pan over medium heat, add 2 quarts water. Bring the water to a boil and add the spaghetti noodles. Boil for 6-7 minutes or until the noodles are tender. Remove the pan from the heat and drain all the water from the noodles.

In a skillet over medium heat, add the butter, green onions and mushrooms. Saute for 4 minutes. Add the ham and turkey to the skillet. Stir constantly and cook for 3 minutes. Remove the skillet from the heat.

Preheat the oven to 350°. Spray a 9 x 13 baking dish with non stick cooking spray. Add the cottage cheese, sour cream, milk, salt, celery salt and black pepper to the casserole dish. Stir until well combined. Add the spaghetti noodles and ham filling from the skillet to the casserole dish. Toss until combined.

Cover the dish with aluminum foil or a lid. Bake for 45 minutes. Remove the aluminum foil and sprinkle the cheddar cheese over the top. Bake for 5 minutes. Remove the casserole from the oven and serve.

Turkey Noodle Bake

Makes 8 servings

Ingredients

2 lbs. ground turkey
2 cups chopped celery
1/4 cup chopped green bell pepper
1/4 cup chopped onion
2 tbs. olive oil
10.75 oz. can cream of mushroom soup
1/4 cup soy sauce
8 oz. can sliced water chestnuts, drained
4 oz. jar sliced mushrooms, drained
1 tsp. salt
1/2 tsp. lemon pepper seasoning
6 oz. pkg. egg noodles
1 cup sour cream

Directions

In a dutch oven over medium heat, add the ground turkey, celery, green bell pepper, onion and olive oil. Stir frequently to break the meat into crumbles as it cooks. Cook about 8 minutes or until the turkey is browned and no longer pink. Drain off the excess grease.

Add the cream of mushroom soup, soy sauce, water chestnuts, mushrooms, salt and lemon pepper seasoning to the pan. Stir until well combined. Reduce the heat to low and simmer for 20 minutes. Stir frequently to keep the sauce combined as it cooks. Remove the pan from the heat.

While the sauce is simmering, cook the egg noodles. In a large sauce pan over medium heat, add 8 cups water. Bring the water to a boil and add the egg noodles. Boil for 6-7 minutes or until the noodles are tender. Remove the pan from the heat and drain all the water from the noodles.

Preheat the oven to 350°. Spray a 9 x 13 baking pan with non stick cooking spray. Add the noodles, turkey sauce and sour cream to the baking dish. Stir until well combined. Bake for 30-40 minutes or until the casserole is hot and bubbly. Remove the casserole from the oven and serve.

Turkey Stroganoff Casserole

Makes 6 servings

Ingredients

8 oz. pkg. egg noodles
2 cups sliced fresh mushrooms
1/2 cup chopped onion
1 garlic clove, minced
2 tbs. unsalted butter
1 lb. ground turkey
10.75 oz. can cream of celery soup
1 tbs. dry sherry
1/2 tsp. salt
1/2 tsp. dried dill
1/2 tsp. paprika
1/8 tsp. cayenne pepper
1 cup sour cream

Directions

In a large sauce pan over medium heat, add 10 cups water. Bring the water to a boil and add the egg noodles. Boil for 6-7 minutes or until the noodles are tender. Remove the pan from the heat and drain all the water from the noodles.

In a skillet over medium heat, add the mushrooms, onion, garlic, butter and ground turkey. Stir frequently to break the meat into crumbles as it cooks. Cook about 7 minutes or until the turkey is well browned and no longer pink. Remove the skillet from the heat and drain off the excess grease.

Add the cream of celery soup, sherry, salt, dill, paprika, cayenne pepper and sour cream to the skillet. Stir until well combined. Preheat the oven to 350°. Spray a 2 quart casserole dish with non stick cooking spray. Add the noodles and turkey sauce to the casserole dish. Toss until well combined.

Bake for 20 minutes or until the casserole is hot and bubbly. Remove the dish from the oven and serve.

Leftover Turkey Casserole

Makes 6 servings

Ingredients

7 oz. pkg. spaghetti noodles
1 3/4 cups shredded Monterey Jack cheese
1 1/2 cups cooked chopped turkey
2 oz. jar diced red pimento, drained
1 green bell pepper, chopped
1 onion, chopped
10.75 oz. can cream of celery soup
1/2 cup chicken broth
1/2 tsp. salt
1/4 tsp. black pepper

Directions

In a large sauce pan over medium heat, add 2 quarts water. Bring the water to a boil and add the spaghetti noodles. Boil for 6-7 minutes or until the noodles are tender. Remove the pan from the heat and drain all the water from the noodles.

Preheat the oven to 350°. Spray a 11 x 7 casserole dish with non stick cooking spray. Add 1 1/4 cups Monterey Jack cheese, turkey, red pimento, green bell pepper, onion, cream of celery soup, chicken broth, salt and black pepper to the spaghetti noodles. Toss until combined.

Spoon the noodles into the prepared casserole dish. Bake for 30 minutes. Sprinkle 1/2 cup Monterey Jack cheese over the top. Bake for 5 minutes. Remove the casserole from the oven and serve.

Hot Brown Pasta Casserole

Makes 4 servings

Ingredients

2 1/2 cups penne pasta
6 oz. cooked ham, cut into 1/2" strips
6 oz. cooked turkey, cut into 1/2" strips
10.75 oz. can condensed cheddar cheese soup
1/2 cup whole milk
1/4 tsp. black pepper
8 tomato slices
8 bacon slices, cooked
1/4 cup freshly grated Parmesan cheese

Directions

In a large sauce pan over medium heat, add 2 quarts water. Bring the water to a boil and add the penne pasta. Boil for 6-7 minutes or until the pasta is tender. Remove the pan from the heat and drain all the water from the pasta.

Preheat the oven to 350°. Spray a 2 quart casserole dish with non stick cooking spray. Add the ham, turkey, cheddar cheese soup, milk and black pepper to the penne pasta. Stir until combined. Spoon the pasta into the prepared casserole dish. Place the tomato slices on top of the casserole dish.

Bake for 15 minutes or until the casserole is hot and bubbly. Place the bacon slices over the casserole dish. Sprinkle the Parmesan cheese over the bacon. Bake for 10 minutes. Remove the casserole from the oven and serve.

Turkey Olive Casserole

This is so easy, delicious and quick to make.

Makes 4 servings

Ingredients

4 oz. uncooked egg noodles
10.75 oz. can cream of mushroom soup
1 cup whole milk
2 cups chopped cooked turkey
1/2 cup pimento stuffed olives
3 oz. can french fried onion rings

Directions

In a large sauce pan over medium heat, add 6 cups water. Bring the water to a boil and add the egg noodles. Boil for 6-7 minutes or until the noodles are tender. Remove the pan from the heat and drain all the water from the noodles.

Preheat the oven to 350°. Spray a 10 x 6 x 2 casserole dish with non stick cooking spray. Add the cream of mushroom soup, milk, turkey, olives and half the onion rings to the egg noodles. Toss until combined. Spoon the noodles into the prepared casserole dish.

Cover the dish with aluminum foil or a lid. Bake for 25 minutes. Remove the aluminum foil and sprinkle the remaining onion rings over the top of the casserole. Bake for 10 minutes or until the casserole is hot, bubbly and the onion rings lightly browned. Remove the dish from the oven and serve.

Chicken Lasagna Bake

Makes 12 servings

Ingredients

8 oz. penne pasta
10.75 oz. can cream of chicken soup
1 cup chicken broth
1/2 tsp. salt
6 oz. cream cheese, softened
1 cup cottage cheese
1/2 cup sour cream
1/2 cup mayonnaise
1/3 cup chopped onion
1/3 cup chopped green bell pepper
1/3 cup pimento stuffed green olives, drained
1/4 cup chopped fresh parsley
3 cups cooked chopped chicken
1/2 cup fine dry breadcrumbs
1 tbs. melted unsalted butter

Directions

In a large sauce pan over medium heat, add 2 quarts water. Bring the water to a boil and add the penne pasta. Boil for 7-8 minutes or until the pasta is tender. Remove the pan from the heat and drain all the water from the pasta.

In a mixing bowl, add the cream of chicken soup, chicken broth and salt. Whisk until well combined. In a separate mixing bowl, add the cream cheese, cottage cheese, sour cream and mayonnaise. Using a mixer on medium speed, beat until well combined and smooth.

Turn the mixer off. Add the onion, green bell pepper, olives and parsley. Stir until well combined.

Preheat the oven to 350°. Spray a 9 x 13 casserole dish with non stick cooking spray. Add the penne pasta to the cream of chicken soup sauce. Stir until combined. Add the chicken and cream cheese mixture to the penne pasta and toss until well combined. Spoon into the casserole dish. Sprinkle the breadcrumbs over the top. Drizzle the melted butter over the breadcrumbs. Bake for 30 minutes or until the dish is hot and bubbly. Remove from the oven and serve.

Chicken Spaghetti Casserole

Makes 8 servings

Ingredients

4 lb. whole fryer chicken
1 bay leaf
Salt to taste and season
8 oz. spaghetti noodles
1 large onion, chopped
1/2 cup green bell pepper, chopped
2 stalks celery, chopped
2 garlic cloves, minced
3 tbs. unsalted butter
10.75 oz. can cream of mushroom soup
29 oz. can diced tomatoes, drained
1 tsp. Worcestershire sauce
4 drops Tabasco sauce
1/8 tsp. black pepper
1 cup shredded cheddar cheese

Directions

In a large dutch oven over medium heat, add the chicken, bay leaf and 1 teaspoon salt. Cover the chicken with water and bring to a boil. When the water is boiling, reduce the heat to medium low and place a lid on the pot. Simmer the chicken about 2 hours or until done and tender. Add water if needed to keep the chicken covered in water. Remove the pan from the heat. Remove the chicken from the pot and set aside to cool. Discard the bay leaf.

When the chicken is cool, remove the meat from the skin and bones. Cut the chicken into bite size pieces. Remove 1/4 cup chicken broth from the pot. Place the chicken broth back on the stove over medium heat and bring to a boil. Break the spaghetti noodles into thirds and place the noodles in the boiling broth. Cook about 7 minutes or until the noodles are tender. Remove the pot from the heat and drain all the broth from the noodles.

In a skillet over medium heat, add the onion, green bell pepper, celery, garlic and butter. Saute the vegetables for 5 minutes. Remove the skillet from the heat and stir in the cream of mushroom soup and 1/4 cup reserved chicken broth. Add to the noodles and stir until combined. Add the chicken, tomatoes, Worcestershire sauce, Tabasco sauce, black pepper and salt to taste to the noodles. Stir until combined.

Preheat the oven to 350°. Spray a 9 x 13 baking dish with non stick cooking spray. Spoon the casserole into dish. Bake for 20 minutes. Sprinkle the cheddar cheese over the top of the casserole. Bake for 5 minutes. Remove the dish from the oven and cool for 5 minutes before serving.

Chicken Vegetable Spaghetti Casserole

Makes 6 servings

Ingredients

4 boneless skinless chicken breast, 6 oz. each
2 tbs. olive oil
3 zucchini, diced
1 green bell pepper, chopped
2 cups sliced fresh mushrooms
1/2 cup chopped onion
1 garlic clove, minced
12 oz. spaghetti noodles
30 oz. jar spaghetti sauce
2 cups shredded mozzarella cheese
2 tbs. chopped fresh parsley

Directions

In a large skillet over medium heat, add the chicken breast and olive oil. Cook about 8 minutes or until the chicken is well browned and no longer pink. Remove the chicken from the skillet but leave the pan drippings in the skillet.

Add the zucchini, green bell pepper, mushrooms, onion and garlic to the skillet. Saute the vegetables for 5 minutes. Add the chicken to the vegetables and cook for 3 minutes. Remove the skillet from the heat.

In a large sauce pan over medium heat, add 12 cups water. Bring the water to a boil and add the spaghetti noodles. Boil for 6-7 minutes or until the noodles are tender. Remove the pan from the heat and drain all the water from the noodles.

Preheat the oven to 350°. Spray a 3 quart casserole dish with non stick cooking spray. Add the chicken and vegetables, spaghetti sauce and 1 cup mozzarella cheese to the noodles. Stir until combined. Spoon the noodles into the casserole dish. Bake for 20 minutes or until hot and bubbly. Sprinkle 1 cup mozzarella cheese and the parsley over the top. Bake for 10 minutes. Remove the casserole from the oven and serve.

Chicken Superb Casserole

Makes 8 servings

Ingredients

3 lbs. meaty chicken pieces (breast, leg, thigh)
8 oz. pkg. egg noodles
1/4 cup plus 2 tbs. unsalted butter
1/4 cup plus 2 tbs. all purpose flour
2 cups half and half
2 tbs. sherry
1 tsp. salt
1/2 tsp. celery salt
1/4 tsp. dried marjoram
1/8 tsp. Beau Monde seasoning
6 oz. jar sliced mushrooms, drained
1/2 cup slivered almonds, toasted
3 tbs. minced fresh parsley
1/2 cup shredded cheddar cheese

Directions

In a large sauce pan over medium heat, add the chicken. Cover the chicken with water and bring the water to a boil. Place a lid on the pan and simmer about 45 minutes or until the chicken is no longer pink and tender. Remove the pan from the heat. Remove the chicken from the pan and set aside to cool. Reserve 2 cups chicken broth and discard the remaining broth.

When the chicken is cool, remove the meat from the bone and skin. Cut the chicken into bite size pieces. In a large sauce pan over medium heat, add 8 cups water. Bring the water to a boil and add the egg noodles. Boil for 6-7 minutes or until the noodles are tender. Remove the pan from the heat and drain all the water from the pasta.

In a large heavy sauce pan over medium heat, add the butter. When the butter melts, add the all purpose flour. Stir constantly and cook for 2 minutes. Slowly whisk in 2 cups reserved chicken broth, half and half, sherry, salt, celery salt, marjoram and Beau Monde seasoning. Stir constantly and cook until the sauce thickens and bubbles. Remove the pan from the heat.

Preheat the oven to 350°. Spray a 9 x 13 baking dish with non stick cooking spray. Add the chicken, noodles, mushrooms, almonds and parsley to the casserole dish. Stir until combined. Pour the sauce over the noodles. Toss until combined. Bake for 35 minutes. Sprinkle the cheddar cheese over the top of the casserole. Bake for 5 minutes. Remove the casserole from the oven and serve.

Pesto Chicken and Pasta Casserole

Makes 4 servings

Ingredients

1 lb. boneless skinless chicken breast
1 tbs. vegetable oil
1 cup sliced fresh mushrooms
14 oz. can diced tomatoes, drained
1 cup chicken broth
1 tbs. cornstarch
8 oz. fettuccine noodles
3 tbs. pesto sauce
Salt and black pepper to taste

Directions

Cut the chicken breast into bite size pieces. In a skillet over medium heat, add the vegetable oil. When the oil is hot, add the chicken breast. Brown the chicken for 5-7 minutes or until the chicken is almost done. Add the mushrooms, tomatoes, chicken broth and cornstarch. Stir frequently and cook until the liquid thickens and the chicken is no longer pink and tender. Remove the skillet from the heat.

While the chicken is cooking, cook the fettuccine noodles. In a large sauce pan over medium heat, add 10 cups water. Bring the water to a boil and add the noodles. Boil for 8-10 minutes or until the noodles are tender. Remove the pan from the heat and drain all the water from the noodles.

Preheat the oven to 350°. Spray a 2 quart casserole dish with non stick cooking spray. Add the noodles, pesto sauce and chicken filling to the casserole dish. Stir until well combined. Season to taste with salt and black pepper. Bake for 20 minutes or until the casserole is hot and bubbly. Remove the dish from the oven and serve.

Szechuan Noodle Skillet

Makes 6 servings

Ingredients

8 oz. pkg. thin spaghetti noodles
1/4 cup sesame oil
1/4 cup soy sauce
2 tbs. rice vinegar
1 1/2 tsp. crushed red pepper flakes
1 tsp. minced fresh ginger
2 large red bell peppers, julienned
4 green onions, cut into 1" pieces
1 garlic clove, minced
10 oz. pkg. fresh spinach, torn into bite size pieces
2 cups cubed cooked chicken
8 oz. can sliced water chestnuts, drained

Directions

In a large sauce pan over medium heat, add 10 cups water. Bring the water to a boil and add the spaghetti. Boil for 6-7 minutes or until the noodles are tender. Remove the pan from the heat and drain all the water from the noodles. Add 2 tablespoons sesame oil, soy sauce, rice vinegar, red pepper flakes and ginger to the noodles. Toss until the noodles are coated with the sesame oil and seasonings.

In a large skillet over medium heat, add 2 tablespoons sesame oil. When the oil is hot, add the red bell pepper, green onions and garlic. Saute the vegetables for 3 minutes. Stir in the spinach and place a lid on the skillet. Cook for 3 minutes.

Add the spaghetti noodles, chicken and water chestnuts to the skillet. Toss until blended. Place the lid on the skillet and cook for 5 minutes or until the chicken is hot. Remove the skillet from the heat and serve.

Roasted Pepper & Broccoli Pasta Skillet

Makes 6 servings

Ingredients

12 oz. pkg. small shell pasta
8 oz. jar roasted red peppers, drained and cut into thin strips
2/3 cup pine nuts
1/2 cup olive oil
1/2 cup chopped fresh parsley
3 cups fresh broccoli, chopped
1 cup freshly grated Parmesan cheese
1/8 tsp. cayenne pepper
1/8 tsp. black pepper

Directions

In a large sauce pan over medium heat, add 10 cups water. Bring the water to a boil and add the shell pasta. Boil for 6-7 minutes or until the pasta is tender. Remove the pan from the heat and drain all the water from the pasta.

In a large skillet over medium heat, add the roasted red peppers, pine nuts, olive oil and parsley. Stir constantly and cook until the pine nuts are toasted. Add the broccoli and cook for 5 minutes. Add the pasta, Parmesan cheese, cayenne pepper and black pepper. Toss until well combined. Cook only until the cheese begins to melt. Remove the skillet from the heat and serve.

Overnight Macaroni & Chicken Casserole

Makes 6 servings

Ingredients

1 cup uncooked elbow macaroni
1 cup diced cooked chicken
10.75 oz. can cream of mushroom soup
1 cup whole milk
4 oz. Velveeta cheese, diced
2 hard boiled eggs, chopped
2 tbs. chopped red pimento

Directions

Spray a 1 1/2 quart casserole with non stick cooking spray. Add all the ingredients to the casserole dish. Stir until combined. Cover the casserole dish with aluminum foil or a lid. Refrigerate the casserole overnight or at least 8 hours.

Remove the casserole from the refrigerator and allow the casserole to sit at room temperature for 1 hour. Leave the aluminum foil or lid on the casserole while cooking. Preheat the oven to 350°. Bake for 1 hour or until the casserole is hot, bubbly and the macaroni tender. Remove from the oven and serve.

Oven Baked Shrimp Stroganoff

Makes 6 servings

Ingredients

8 oz. pkg. egg noodles
1 cup sour cream
10.75 oz. can cream of mushroom soup
1 tsp. dried dill
1/4 cup sliced green onion
1/4 cup sliced black olives
1 cup shredded cheddar cheese
1 lb. shrimp, peeled and deveined

Directions

In a large sauce pan over medium heat, add 10 cups water. Bring the water to a boil and add the egg noodles. Boil for 6-7 minutes or until the noodles are tender. Remove the pan from the heat and drain all the water from the noodles.

In a mixing bowl, add the sour cream, cream of mushroom soup, dill, green onion, black olives, 1/2 cup cheddar cheese and shrimp. Stir until well combined. Add the noodles and toss until combined.

Preheat the oven to 350°. Spray a 2 quart casserole dish with non stick cooking spray. Add the noodles to the dish. Cover the dish with aluminum foil or a lid. Bake for 30 minutes or until the shrimp are pink and tender. Remove the aluminum foil and sprinkle 1/2 cup cheddar cheese over the top of the casserole. Bake for 5 minutes or until the casserole is hot and bubbly. Remove the dish from the oven and serve.

Seafood Manicotti Casserole

Makes 6 servings

Ingredients

1 quart whipping cream
1/2 tsp. salt
1/4 tsp. black pepper
1/4 tsp. cayenne pepper
14 manicotti shells
3 tbs. unsalted butter
1 cup chopped onion
1 cup chopped green bell pepper
1/4 cup chopped celery
1 garlic clove, minced
2 lbs. fresh shrimp, peeled and deveined
1 lb. fresh crab meat, drained and flaked
1/2 cup shredded cheddar cheese
1/2 cup shredded Pepper Jack cheese

Directions

In a large sauce pan over medium heat, add the whipping cream, salt, black pepper and cayenne pepper. Stir constantly and cook for 30 minutes. The cream should be reduced to about 2 cups. Remove the pan from the heat.

In a large sauce pan over medium heat, add 2 quarts water. Bring the water to a boil and add the manicotti shells. Boil for 7-8 minutes or until the shells are tender. Remove the pan from the heat and drain all the water from the shells. Rinse the shells with cold water and drain all the water from the shells again.

In a large skillet over medium heat, add the butter, onion, green bell pepper, celery and garlic. Saute the vegetables for 5 minutes. Add the shrimp and crab meat to the skillet. Stir constantly and cook about 5 minutes or until the shrimp turn pink. Remove the skillet from the heat and cool for 10 minutes. Drain the skillet of any liquid.

Add the whipping cream to the seafood filling and stir until combined. Fill the manicotti shells with the seafood filling. Preheat the oven to 350°. Spray a 9 x 13 baking dish with non stick cooking spray. Place the manicotti shells in the baking dish. Sprinkle the cheddar cheese and Pepper Jack cheese over the top of the shells. Cover the dish with aluminum foil and bake for 15 minutes. Remove the aluminum foil and bake for 10 minutes. Remove the dish from the oven and serve.

Crab Meat Lasagna

Makes 8 servings

Ingredients

6 oz. egg noodles
1/4 cup unsalted butter
1 cup shredded carrot
1/2 cup finely chopped celery
1/2 cup finely chopped onion
1/3 cup finely chopped yellow bell pepper
1/3 cup finely chopped red bell pepper
3 garlic cloves, minced
1 tsp. coriander seeds, crushed
8 oz. carton plain yogurt
1/4 cup chopped fresh cilantro
1/4 tsp. salt
1/8 tsp. black pepper
1/8 tsp. ground nutmeg
1 lb. fresh crab meat, diced
2 cups shredded mozzarella cheese
2 cups shredded American cheese

Directions

In a large sauce pan over medium heat, add 2 quarts water. Bring the water to a boil and add the egg noodles. Boil for 6-7 minutes or until the noodles are tender. Remove the pan from the heat and drain all the water from the noodles.

While the noodles are cooking, cook the vegetables. In a skillet over medium heat, add the butter, carrot, celery, onion, yellow bell pepper, red bell pepper and garlic. Saute the vegetables for 5 minutes. Add the coriander seeds and cook for 3 minutes. Remove the skillet from the heat.

Add the yogurt, cilantro, salt, black pepper, nutmeg, crab meat and mozzarella cheese to the skillet. Stir until combined. Preheat the oven to 350°. Spray a 9 x 13 baking dish with non stick cooking spray. Add the noodles and crab filling to the casserole dish. Toss until blended.

Cover the dish with aluminum foil and bake for 30 minutes. Remove the aluminum foil and sprinkle the American cheese over the top. Bake for 5 minutes. Remove the dish from the oven and serve.

Shrimp Noodle Casserole

Makes 6 servings

Ingredients

14 cups water
2 lbs. fresh shrimp
8 oz. pkg. egg noodles
1/2 cup sliced green onions
1/4 cup chopped green bell pepper
2 tbs. unsalted butter
2 cans cream of mushroom soup, 10.75 oz. size
8 oz. carton plain yogurt
1/2 cup shredded cheddar cheese
1/2 tsp. dried dill
1/2 tsp. black pepper
1/4 tsp. salt

Directions

Add 6 cups water to a large sauce pan over medium heat. Bring the water to a boil and add the shrimp. Cook for 5 minutes or until the shrimp turn pink. Remove the pan from the heat and drain all the water from the shrimp. Rinse the shrimp in cold water and drain the water again.

Peel and devein the shrimp. Chop half the shrimp into bite size pieces. Leave the remaining shrimp whole. In a large sauce pan over medium heat, add 8 cups water. Bring the water to a boil and add the egg noodles. Boil for 6-7 minutes or until the noodles are tender. Remove the pan from the heat and drain all the water from the pasta.

In a large deep skillet, add the green onions, green bell pepper and butter. Saute the vegetables for 5 minutes. Add the cream of mushroom soup, yogurt, cheddar cheese, dill, black pepper and salt. Stir until well combined. Cook only until the sauce is hot and the cheese melted. Stir in the noodles and chopped shrimp. Remove the skillet from the heat.

Preheat the oven to 350°. Spoon the filling into a 3 quart casserole dish. Place the whole shrimp on top. Cover the dish with aluminum foil or a lid. Bake for 30 minutes. Remove the casserole from the oven and serve.

Shrimp Feta Vermicelli

Makes 4 servings

Ingredients

1/4 cup olive oil
1/8 tsp. crushed red pepper flakes
1 lb. shrimp, peeled and deveined
2/3 cup crumbled feta cheese
1/2 tsp. crushed garlic
14 oz. can diced tomatoes
1/4 cup dry white wine
3/4 tsp. dried basil
1/2 tsp. dried oregano
1/4 tsp. salt
1/4 tsp. black pepper
8 oz. vermicelli
2 tbs. chopped fresh basil

Directions

In a large deep skillet over medium heat, add 2 tablespoons olive oil, red pepper flakes and shrimp. Saute the shrimp for 2 minutes. The shrimp will not be cooked but should be light pink. Remove the shrimp from the skillet and place in a 10 x 6 x 2 baking dish. Sprinkle the feta cheese over the shrimp. Preheat the oven to 400°.

Add the remaining olive oil and garlic to the skillet. Reduce the heat to low and saute the garlic for 2 minutes. Add the tomatoes with juice and cook for 1 minute. Add the white wine, basil, oregano, salt and black pepper. Stir until combined and simmer the sauce for 10 minutes. Remove the skillet from the heat and pour the sauce over the shrimp. Bake for 10 minutes. The shrimp should be done and the sauce bubbly. Remove the dish from the oven .

In a large sauce pan over medium heat, add 8 cups water. Bring the water to a boil and add the vermicelli. Boil for 6-7 minutes or until the vermicelli is tender. Remove the pan from the heat and drain all the water from the pasta. Add the vermicelli to the shrimp casserole and toss until combined. Sprinkle the basil over the top before serving.

Scalloped Oyster Macaroni Casserole

Makes 4 servings

Ingredients

1 cup elbow macaroni
12 saltine crackers, broken into small pieces
1 pint oysters, drained
1/2 tsp. salt
1/4 tsp. black pepper
1 cup whole milk
1/4 cup unsalted butter
1/4 cup saltine cracker crumbs

Directions

In a large sauce pan over medium heat, add 8 cups water. Bring the water to a boil and add the macaroni. Boil for 6-7 minutes or until the macaroni is tender. Remove the pan from the heat and drain all the water from the macaroni.

Preheat the oven to 350°. Spray a 1 1/2 quart casserole dish with non stick cooking spray. Sprinkle half the broken crackers in the bottom of the casserole dish. Spoon half the oysters and 1/2 the macaroni over the crackers. Sprinkle 1/4 teaspoon salt and 1/8 teaspoon black pepper over the oysters and macaroni.

Repeat the layering process one more time. Pour the milk over the top of the oysters and macaroni. Do not stir. Cut the butter into small pieces and place over the top of the casserole. Sprinkle the saltine cracker crumbs over the top of the dish.

Bake for 45 minutes or until the casserole is hot, bubbly and the cracker crumbs golden brown. The oysters should be fully cooked. Remove from the oven and serve.

Crawfish Pasta Casserole

Makes 6 servings

Ingredients

7 oz. egg noodles
2 tbs. unsalted butter
1 green bell pepper, chopped
1 onion, chopped
1 celery stalk, chopped
4 garlic cloves, minced
2 tbs. all purpose flour
1 lb. Velveeta cheese, cubed
1 lb. peeled and cooked crawfish tails
1 cup half and half
2 tbs. chopped jalapeno pepper
1/4 cup shredded Parmesan cheese

Directions

In a large sauce pan over medium heat, add 8 cups water. Bring the water to a boil and add the egg noodles. Boil for 6-7 minutes or until the noodles are tender. Remove the pan from the heat and drain all the water from the noodles.

In a dutch oven, add the butter, green bell pepper, onion, celery and garlic. Saute the vegetables for 10 minutes. Sprinkle the all purpose flour over the vegetables. Stir constantly and cook for 1 minute or until the flour is smooth. Add the Velveeta cheese, crawfish tails, half and half and jalapeno pepper. Stir until well combined and the cheese melts.

Add the egg noodles and toss until well blended. Remove the pan from the heat. Preheat the oven to 350°. Spray a 11 x 7 baking dish with non stick cooking spray. Spoon the noodle filling into the casserole dish. Sprinkle the Parmesan cheese over the top. Bake for 30 minutes or until hot and bubbly. Remove the dish from the oven and serve.

Three Cheese Ziti Casserole

Makes 8 servings

Ingredients

12 oz. pkg. ziti noodles
3 cups marinara sauce
2 cups shredded mozzarella cheese
1 cup freshly grated Parmesan cheese
1 cup ricotta cheese
3 tbs. prepared pesto sauce
1/4 tsp. crushed red pepper flakes

Directions

In a large sauce pan over medium heat, add 12 cups water. Bring the water to a boil and add the ziti noodles. Boil for 6-7 minutes or until the noodles are tender. Remove the pan from the heat and drain all the water from the noodles.

Add 2 cups marinara sauce, 1 cup mozzarella cheese, 1/2 cup Parmesan cheese, ricotta cheese, pesto sauce and red pepper flakes to the ziti noodles. Toss until combined. Spray a 9 x 13 casserole dish with non stick cooking spray. Preheat the oven to 400°. Spread the noodles into the casserole dish.

Spoon 1 cup marinara sauce over the noodles. Sprinkle 1 cup mozzarella cheese and 1/2 cup Parmesan cheese over the top. Bake for 30 minutes or until the casserole is hot and the cheeses melted and bubbly. Remove the dish from the oven and serve.

Four Cheese Pasta Bake

Makes 6 servings

Ingredients

32 jumbo pasta shells
8 oz. pkg. cream cheese, softened
1 cup cottage cheese
1 cup shredded mozzarella cheese
1 egg, beaten
1/4 grated Parmesan cheese
2 tbs. chopped fresh parsley
2 tsp. dried basil
1 1/2 tsp. dried oregano
1 1/2 tsp. dried thyme
1/8 tsp. grated lemon zest
Pinch of ground nutmeg
14 oz. can stewed tomatoes
8 oz. can tomato sauce
1 cup white wine or chicken broth
8 oz. can sliced mushrooms
1 garlic clove, minced

Directions

In a large sauce pan over medium heat, add 12 cups water. Bring the water to a boil and add the pasta shells. Boil for 8-10 minutes or until the shells are tender. Remove the pan from the heat and drain all the water from the pasta. Rinse the pasta shells with cold water and drain all the water from the shells.

In a mixing bowl, add the cream cheese, cottage cheese, mozzarella cheese, egg, Parmesan cheese, parsley, basil, 1/2 teaspoon oregano, 1/2 teaspoon thyme, lemon zest and nutmeg. Stir until well combined. Spoon the cheese filling into the pasta shells. Place the shells in a 12 x 8 x 2 baking dish.

Preheat the oven to 350°. Bake for 25 minutes. In a sauce pan over medium heat, add the tomatoes with juice, tomato sauce, white wine, mushrooms, garlic, 1 teaspoon oregano and 1 teaspoon thyme. Stir frequently and simmer the sauce for 10 minutes. Use a spoon and break the tomatoes up as the sauce cooks. Remove the pan from the heat and pour the sauce over the cooked shells. Cover the dish with aluminum foil. Bake for 20 minutes or until the filling is hot and the cheeses melted. Remove the dish from the oven and serve.

Cheesy Macaroni Mushroom Bake

Makes 6 servings

Ingredients

8 oz. pkg. elbow macaroni
10.75 oz. can cream of celery soup
1 cup whole milk
1/2 cup chopped onion
1 tsp. salt
1/4 tsp. black pepper
1/4 tsp. dried oregano
1 cup sliced cooked mushrooms
2 cups shredded cheddar cheese
3 tbs. grated Parmesan cheese
2 tomatoes, cut into wedges

Directions

In a large sauce pan over medium heat, add 8 cups water. Bring the water to a boil and add the macaroni. Boil for 6-7 minutes or until the macaroni is tender. Remove the pan from the heat and drain all the water from the macaroni.

In a mixing bowl, add the cream of celery soup, milk, onion, salt, black pepper and oregano. Stir until combined. Preheat the oven to 350°. Spray a 2 quart casserole dish with non stick cooking spray.

Spread half the macaroni in the bottom of the casserole dish. Spoon half the soup over the macaroni. Sprinkle 1/2 cup mushrooms and 1 cup shredded cheddar cheese over the soup. Repeat the layering process one more time. Sprinkle the Parmesan cheese over the top of the casserole.

Bake for 30 minutes or until the casserole is hot, bubbly and the cheeses melted. Place the tomatoes on top of the casserole and bake for 5 minutes. Remove the dish from the oven and cool for 5 minutes before serving.

Vegetable Lasagna Casserole

Makes 8 servings

Ingredients

12 oz. rotini pasta
2 cups sliced fresh mushrooms
1 cup grated carrot
1/2 cup chopped onion
1 tbs. olive oil
15 oz. can tomato sauce
12 oz. can tomato paste
1/2 cup sliced black olives
4 oz. can chopped green chiles
1 1/2 tsp. dried oregano
10 oz. pkg. frozen spinach, thawed and drained
2 cups cottage cheese
4 cups shredded Pepper Jack cheese
1/2 cup shredded Parmesan cheese

Directions

In a large sauce pan over medium heat, add 2 quarts water. Bring the water to a boil and add the rotini pasta. Boil for 7-8 minutes or until the pasta is tender. Remove the pan from the heat and drain all the water from the pasta.

While the pasta is cooking, make the sauce. In a large skillet over medium heat, add the mushrooms, carrot, onion and olive oil. Saute the vegetables for 5 minutes. Add the tomato sauce, tomato paste, black olives, green chiles and oregano. Stir constantly and bring the sauce to a boil. Reduce the heat to low and simmer for 10 minutes.

Add the spinach and stir until combined. Remove the skillet from the heat.

Add the cottage cheese and 3 cups Pepper Jack cheese to the pasta. Toss until blended. Preheat the oven to 350°. Spray a 9 x 13 casserole dish with non stick cooking spray. Add the vegetable sauce to the pasta. Toss until combined and spoon into the casserole dish. Sprinkle 1 cup Pepper Jack cheese and the Parmesan cheese over the top of the casserole.

Cover the dish with aluminum foil or a lid. Bake for 45 minutes. Remove the aluminum foil and bake for 10 minutes. The dish should be hot, bubbly and the cheese lightly browned when ready. Remove from the oven and cool for 10 minutes before serving.

Veggie Macaroni Cheese Casserole

Makes 8 servings

Ingredients

8 oz. elbow macaroni
1 cup chopped fresh broccoli
1 cup diced yellow squash
1/2 cup chopped carrot
1 onion, chopped
2 garlic cloves, minced
2 tsp. olive oil
7 oz. jar roasted red bell peppers, drained and chopped
16 oz. container ricotta cheese
12 oz. can evaporated milk
1 tbs. prepared mustard (use your favorite flavor)
1 tsp. salt
1 tsp. black pepper
2 beaten eggs
1 large tomato, sliced
1/2 cup Italian seasoned breadcrumbs
1/2 cup shredded Romano cheese

Directions

In a large sauce pan over medium heat, add 8 cups water. Bring the water to a boil and add the macaroni. Boil for 6-7 minutes or until the macaroni is tender. Remove the pan from the heat and drain all the water from the macaroni.

In a dutch oven, add the broccoli, squash, carrot, onion, garlic and olive oil. Saute the vegetables for 5 minutes. Add the macaroni, red bell peppers, ricotta cheese, evaporated milk, mustard, salt, black pepper and eggs. Stir until well combined and remove the pan from the heat.

Preheat the oven to 350°. Spray a 9 x 13 casserole dish with non stick cooking spray. Spoon the noodle filling into the casserole dish. Sprinkle the tomato, breadcrumbs and Romano cheese over the top of the casserole. Cover the dish with aluminum foil or a lid. Bake for 20 minutes. Remove the aluminum foil and cook for 15 minutes or until hot and bubbly.

Vegetable Noodle Casserole

Makes 6 servings

Ingredients

4 oz. egg noodles
1 stalk celery, sliced
1 onion, chopped
1 green bell pepper, chopped
1 cup chopped fresh broccoli
2 tbs. vegetable oil
1/2 cup whole milk
1/4 tsp. salt
1/4 tsp. black pepper
1 1/2 cups shredded Monterey Jack cheese
3 tbs. dry breadcrumbs
1 tbs. unsalted butter, melted

Directions

In a large sauce pan over medium heat, add 8 cups water. Bring the water to a boil and add the egg noodles. Boil for 6-7 minutes or until the noodles are tender. Remove the pan from the heat and drain all the water from the noodles.

In a skillet over medium heat, add the celery, onion, green bell pepper, broccoli and vegetable oil. Saute the vegetables about 5 minutes or until tender. Add the milk, salt, black pepper and Monterey Jack cheese. Stir only until combined and remove the skillet from the heat.

Preheat the oven to 350°. Add the egg noodles and vegetables from the skillet to to a 1 1/2 quart baking dish. Stir until combined. Cover the dish with aluminum foil or a lid. Bake for 15 minutes or until the casserole is hot. Remove the aluminum foil and sprinkle the breadcrumbs over the top of the casserole. Drizzle the melted butter over the breadcrumbs. Bake for 10 minutes or until the breadcrumbs are golden brown. Remove the dish from the oven and serve.

Avocado Vegetable Lasagna Casserole

Makes 8 servings

Ingredients

2 cartons ricotta cheese, 15 oz. size
12 oz. shredded Italian cheese blend
3 eggs
1/4 cup chopped fresh basil
1/4 tsp. cayenne pepper
1 tsp. salt
1 tsp. black pepper
6 oz. jar marinated artichoke hearts, chopped
4 green onions, sliced
3 large avocados, chopped
12 oz. egg noodles
2 tbs. unsalted butter
2 garlic cloves, minced
2 tbs. all purpose flour
2 cups whipping cream
1 1/2 cups shredded Parmesan cheese

Directions

In a mixing bowl, add the ricotta cheese, Italian cheese blend, eggs, basil, cayenne pepper, 1/2 teaspoon salt and 1/2 teaspoon black pepper. Stir until well blended.

Drain the artichokes but save the marinade. In a separate bowl, add the artichokes, marinade, green onions, avocados, 1/2 teaspoon salt and 1/2 teaspoon black pepper. Stir until well combined.

In a large sauce pan over medium heat, add 12 cups water. Bring the water to a boil and add the egg noodles. Boil for 6-7 minutes or until the noodles are tender. Remove the pan from the heat and drain all the water from the noodles.

While the noodles are cooking, add the butter and garlic to a sauce pan over medium heat. Saute the garlic for 4 minutes. Sprinkle the all purpose flour over the garlic and cook for 1 minute. Stir constantly and add the whipping cream. Cook until the sauce thickens and just begins to bubble. Remove the pan from the heat and stir in 1 cup Parmesan cheese.

Preheat the oven to 350°. Spray a 9 x 13 baking pan with non stick cooking spray. Spread half the noodles in the bottom of the baking pan. Spread half the ricotta cheese sauce over the noodles. Spread half the avocado topping over the ricotta cheese. Spoon half the Parmesan cheese sauce over the avocado topping. Repeat the layering process one more time.

Sprinkle the remaining 1/2 cup Parmesan cheese over the top. Cover the dish with aluminum foil and bake for 40 minutes. Remove the aluminum foil and bake for 5 minutes or until hot, bubbly and the cheeses melted. Remove the dish from the oven and cool for 5 minutes before serving.

Four Cheese Noodle Casserole

Makes 8 servings

Ingredients

1 lb. pkg. wide egg noodles
15 oz. container ricotta cheese
1 cup grated Parmesan cheese
1 cup whipping cream
3/4 cup shredded Swiss cheese
3/4 cup shredded mozzarella cheese
1 egg, beaten
3 slices mozzarella cheese, about 1 oz. each, cut in half

Directions

In a large sauce pan over medium heat, add 12 cups water. Bring the water to a boil and add the egg noodles. Boil for 6-7 minutes or until the egg noodles are tender. Remove the pan from the heat and drain all the water from the noodles.

Preheat the oven to 400°. Spray a 11 x 7 casserole dish with non stick cooking spray. Add the noodles, ricotta cheese, Parmesan cheese, whipping cream, Swiss cheese, shredded mozzarella cheese and egg to the casserole dish. Stir until well combined.

Bake for 20 minutes or until the dish is hot and bubbly. Place the sliced mozzarella over the top. Bake for 10 minutes or until the mozzarella cheese is melted and lightly browned. Remove the casserole from the oven and cool for 5 minutes before serving.

Baked Summer Veggie Ziti Casserole

Makes 4 servings

Ingredients

4 oz. ziti pasta
1 tbs. olive oil
2 cups chopped yellow squash
1 cup chopped zucchini
1/2 cup chopped onion
2 cups diced fresh tomato
2 garlic cloves, minced
1 cup shredded mozzarella cheese
2 tbs. chopped fresh basil
2 tsp. chopped fresh oregano
1/8 tsp. cayenne pepper
3/4 tsp. salt
1 egg, beaten
1/4 cup ricotta cheese

Directions

In a large sauce pan over medium heat, add 8 cups water. Bring the water to a boil and add the ziti pasta. Boil for 6-7 minutes or until the ziti is tender. Remove the pan from the heat and drain all the water from the pasta.

In a skillet over medium heat, add the olive oil, yellow squash, zucchini and onion. Saute the vegetables for 5 minutes. Add the tomato and garlic. Saute for 3 minutes. Remove the skillet from the heat and stir in the ziti, 1/2 cup mozzarella cheese, basil, oregano, cayenne pepper and salt. Stir until well combined.

In a separate bowl, add the egg and ricotta cheese. Mix until well combined and add to the pasta and vegetables. Toss until combined. Preheat the oven to 350°. Spoon the ziti filling into a 1 1/2 quart casserole dish. Sprinkle 1/2 cup mozzarella cheese over the top of the dish. Bake for 20 minutes or until the casserole is hot and bubbly. Remove the dish from the oven and serve.

Macaroni, Cheese & Tomato Casserole

Makes 6 servings

Ingredients

2 cups elbow macaroni
14 oz. can diced tomatoes
2/3 cup water
8 oz. cheddar cheese, cubed
1/2 tsp. salt
1/4 tsp. black pepper
2 tbs. granulated sugar
6 oz. cheddar cheese slices

Directions

In a large sauce pan over medium heat, add 2 quarts water. Bring the water to a boil and add the elbow macaroni. Boil for 6-7 minutes or until the macaroni is tender. Remove the pan from the heat and drain all the water from the macaroni.

Preheat the oven to 350°. Spray a 2 quart casserole dish with non stick cooking spray. Add the macaroni, tomatoes, water, cubed cheddar cheese, salt, black pepper and granulated sugar to the casserole dish. Stir until combined.

Arrange the cheddar cheese slices over the top. Bake for 35-45 minutes or until the dish is hot, bubbly and the cheddar cheese lightly browned. Remove from the oven and serve.

Garden Primavera Skillet

Makes 4 servings

Ingredients

8 oz. pkg. spinach rotini pasta
2 tbs. olive oil
1/4 cup unsalted butter
1 onion, thinly sliced
1 garlic clove, minced
1 1/2 cups broccoli florets
1 carrot, thinly sliced
2 cups sliced fresh mushrooms
3 tbs. chicken broth
1/2 tsp. dried basil
1/2 tsp. dried parsley
1/4 tsp. black pepper
1/2 cup grated Parmesan cheese

Directions

In a large sauce pan over medium heat, add 10 cups water. Bring the water to a boil and add the rotini pasta. Boil for 6-7 minutes or until the pasta is tender. Remove the pan from the heat and drain all the water from the pasta. Rinse the pasta with cold water and drain all the water from the pasta again.

In a skillet over medium heat, add the olive oil and butter. When the butter melts, add the onion and garlic. Saute for 2 minutes. Add the broccoli and carrot to the skillet. Cook for 2 minutes. Add the mushrooms and cook for 2 minutes. Add the chicken broth, basil, parsley and black pepper. Stir frequently and cook about 5 minutes or until the vegetables are tender.

Add the pasta and Parmesan cheese to the skillet. Stir until well combined and cook only until thoroughly heated. Remove the skillet from the heat and serve.

Red Bell Pepper Pasta Bake

Makes 8 servings

Ingredients

1/4 cup unsalted butter, melted
3 tbs. olive oil
4 garlic cloves, minced
1 tsp. grated lemon zest
1/2 tsp. crushed red pepper flakes
1 3/4 cups chicken broth
3 tbs. lemon juice
1/2 tsp. salt
1/2 tsp. black pepper
1 lb. pkg. fettuccine noodles
2 large red bell peppers, cut into thin strips
Parmesan cheese, optional

Directions

In a large sauce pan over medium heat, add the butter, olive oil, garlic, lemon zest and red pepper flakes. Stir constantly and cook for 2 minutes. Add the chicken broth and lemon juice. Simmer for 20-25 minutes or until the broth has reduced to about 1 1/4 cups. Stir in the salt and black pepper. Remove the pan from the heat.

While the broth is cooking, make the pasta. In a large sauce pan over medium heat, add 12 cups water. Bring the water to a boil and add the fettuccine. Boil for 8-10 minutes or until the fettuccine is tender. Remove the pan from the heat and drain all the water from the pasta. Add the chicken broth sauce and red bell peppers to the fettuccine noodles. Stir until combined and bring to a boil. Cook for 1 minute. Remove the pan from the heat.

Preheat the oven to 350°. Pour the fettuccine with any liquid into a 9 x 13 baking dish. Bake for 15 minutes or until the casserole is hot and bubbly and most of the liquid absorbed. Remove the casserole from the oven and sprinkle the Parmesan cheese over the top if desired.

Sauteed Spaghetti Vegetable Skillet

Makes 4 servings

Ingredients

7 oz. pkg. spaghetti noodles
3 tbs. unsalted butter
1 onion, chopped
2 zucchini, cut into 2" spears
3/4 cup cucumber, peeled and chopped
1/2 cup grated carrot
1/2 cup chopped green bell pepper
2 tomatoes, chopped
3 tbs. minced fresh parsley
Salt and black pepper to taste
1/3 cup grated Parmesan cheese

Directions

In a large sauce pan over medium heat, add 8 cups water. Bring the water to a boil and add the spaghetti. Boil for 6-7 minutes or until the noodles are tender. Remove the pan from the heat and drain all the water from the noodles.

In a large skillet, add the butter and onion. Saute the onion for 3 minutes. Add the zucchini, cucumber, carrot and green bell pepper. Saute the vegetables for 5 minutes. Add the spaghetti noodles, tomatoes and parsley. Stir until combined. Season to taste with salt and black pepper.

Reduce the heat to low and simmer for 5 minutes. Remove the skillet from the heat and sprinkle the Parmesan cheese over the top before serving.

Asparagus Spaghetti Casserole

Makes 6 servings

Ingredients

7 oz. pkg. spaghetti noodles
3 cups fresh asparagus, cut into 1" pieces
1 tsp. unsalted butter
10.75 oz. can cream of mushroom soup
1 cup shredded cheddar cheese
1/2 cup whole milk

Directions

In a large sauce pan over medium heat, add 8 cups water. Bring the water to a boil and add the spaghetti. Boil for 6-7 minutes or until the noodles are tender. Remove the pan from the heat and drain all the water from the noodles.

In a large sauce pan over medium heat, add the asparagus. Cover the asparagus with water and bring to a boil. Cook for 5-6 minutes or until the asparagus is tender. Remove the pan from the heat and drain all the water from the pan. Add the butter and toss until the butter melts.

Preheat the oven to 400°. Spray a 2 quart casserole dish with non stick cooking spray. Place half the spaghetti noodles in the casserole dish. Place 1 1/2 cups asparagus over the noodles. Spread half the cream of mushroom soup over the asparagus. Sprinkle 1/2 cup cheddar cheese over the soup. Repeat the layering process one more time.

Pour the milk over the top of the casserole. Do not stir. Bake for 20 minutes or until the casserole is hot and bubbly. Remove from the oven and serve.

Cheddar Onion Macaroni Casserole

Makes 6 servings

Ingredients

8 oz. pkg. elbow macaroni
10.75 oz. can cream of mushroom soup
1 onion, grated
4 cups shredded cheddar cheese
2 oz. jar chopped red pimento, drained
1 cup mayonnaise
1 cup butter cracker crumbs
3 tbs. unsalted butter, melted

Directions

In a large sauce pan over medium heat, add 8 cups water. Bring the water to a boil and add the macaroni. Boil for 6-7 minutes or until the macaroni is tender. Remove the pan from the heat and drain all the water from the macaroni.

Preheat the oven to 350°. Spray a 12 x 8 x 2 casserole dish with non stick cooking spray. Add the macaroni, cream of mushroom soup, onion, cheddar cheese, red pimento and mayonnaise to the dish. Stir until well combined.

Sprinkle the cracker crumbs over the top of the casserole. Drizzle the melted butter over the top of the cracker crumbs. Bake for 30 minutes or until the casserole is hot, bubbly and the crackers golden brown. Remove from the oven and cool for 5 minutes before serving.

Southwestern Pumpkin Stuffed Shells

Makes 4 servings

Ingredients

18 jumbo pasta shells
16 oz. can pumpkin
1 egg
1/2 cup Italian seasoned breadcrumbs
1/2 cup shredded Parmesan cheese
1/2 tsp. ground nutmeg
16 oz. jar picante sauce
1 cup shredded Pepper Jack cheese
2 tbs. chopped fresh parsley

Directions

In a large sauce pan over medium heat, add 10 cups water. Bring the water to a boil and add the pasta shells. Boil for 8-10 minutes or until the pasta shells are tender. Remove the pan from the heat and drain all the water from the pasta.

In a mixing bowl, add the pumpkin, egg, breadcrumbs, Parmesan cheese and nutmeg. Stir until well combined. Stuff the pasta shells with the pumpkin filling. Preheat the oven to 350°. Spread 1 cup picante sauce in the bottom of a 9 x 13 casserole dish. Place the shells on top of the picante sauce. Spoon the remaining picante sauce over the shells.

Bake for 30 minutes or until the filling is hot and bubbly. Sprinkle the Pepper Jack cheese and parsley over the top of the shells. Bake for

5 minutes. Remove the dish from the oven and cool for 5 minutes before serving.

Spinach Stuffed Shells

Makes 8 servings

Ingredients

2 pkgs. thawed frozen chopped spinach, 10 oz. size
1 tbs. unsalted butter
1 onion, diced
29 oz. can diced tomatoes
6 oz. can tomato paste
8 oz. can tomato sauce
2 tsp. light brown sugar
1/2 tsp. salt
1/2 tsp. black pepper
1 tsp. dried oregano
24 jumbo macaroni shells
16 oz. container cottage cheese
1 cup shredded mozzarella cheese

Directions

Make sure the spinach is drained of all moisture. In a skillet over medium heat, add the butter. When the butter melts, add the onion. Saute for 4 minutes. Add the tomatoes with juice, tomato paste, tomato sauce, brown sugar, salt, 1/4 teaspoon black pepper and oregano. Stir until well combined and bring to a boil. Reduce the heat to low and place a lid on the skillet. Simmer for 20 minutes. Remove the skillet from the heat.

While the sauce is cooking, cook the macaroni shells. In a large stock pot over medium heat, add 10 cups water. When the water boils, add the macaroni shells. Cook for 8-10 minutes or until the shells are tender. Remove the pot from the heat and drain all the water from the shells. Rinse the shells with cold water until cool. Drain all the water from the shells.

Preheat the oven to 350°. Spray a 9 x 13 casserole dish with non stick cooking spray. In a mixing bowl, add the spinach, cottage cheese and 1/4 teaspoon black pepper. Stir until well combined. Fill each shell with 2 tablespoons spinach filling. Place the shells in the baking dish. Pour the sauce over the shells. Sprinkle the mozzarella cheese over the top. Bake for 20 minutes or until the filling is hot and bubbly. Remove from the oven and serve.

Spinach Manicotti Casserole

Makes 6 servings

Ingredients

10 oz. pkg. frozen spinach, thawed
1 tbs. vegetable oil
3/4 cup diced fresh mushrooms
1/4 cup diced onion
3 garlic cloves, minced
1 beaten egg
1/3 cup plus 2 tbs. freshly grated Parmesan cheese
1/2 tsp. dried oregano
1/4 tsp. dried basil
8 cooked manicotti shells
2 tbs. nonfat dry milk powder
1 cup whole milk
1 1/2 tbs. unsalted butter
2 tbs. all purpose flour
1/4 tsp. ground nutmeg
1/4 tsp. black pepper
2 cups spaghetti sauce
2 tbs. chopped fresh parsley

Directions

Press the spinach between paper towels. Remove all the moisture you can from the spinach. In a large skillet over medium heat, add the vegetable oil. When the oil is hot, add the mushrooms, onion and garlic. Saute for 2 minutes. Add the spinach and saute until the mushrooms are tender and all the liquid has evaporated.

Remove the skillet from the heat and cool for 5 minutes. Stir in the beaten egg, 2 tablespoons Parmesan cheese, oregano and basil. Stuff each manicotti shell with the spinach filling.

In a small bowl, stir together the dry milk powder and milk. In a sauce pan over medium heat, add the butter. When the butter melts, add the all purpose flour. Stir constantly and cook for 1 minute. Keep stirring and slowly add the milk. Cook until the sauce thickens and bubbles. Add 1/3 cup Parmesan cheese, nutmeg and black pepper to the pan. Stir constantly and cook until the cheese melts. Remove the pan from the heat.

Preheat the oven to 375°. Spray a 12 x 8 x 2 baking dish with non stick cooking spray. Spread 1 cup spaghetti sauce in the bottom of the dish. Place the stuffed manicotti shells in the baking dish. Spoon the remaining spaghetti sauce over the shells. Spoon the Parmesan cheese sauce down the center of the casserole dish.

Cover the dish with aluminum foil or a lid. Bake for 30 minutes. Remove the dish from the oven and remove the aluminum foil. Sprinkle the parsley over the top before serving.

Spinach Macaroni Bake

Makes 8 servings

Ingredients

8 oz. elbow macaroni, cooked
1 tsp. vegetable oil
4 cups broccoli florets
1 1/2 tsp. salt
6 oz. pkg. fresh baby spinach
2 tbs. unsalted butter
1/2 cup chopped onion
4 cups fresh mushrooms, quartered
2 tbs. all purpose flour
2 cups whole milk
2 cups shredded white cheddar cheese
1 cup whipping cream
1/2 tsp. black pepper
1/2 tsp. ground nutmeg

Directions

In a large bowl, add the macaroni and vegetable oil. Toss until the macaroni is coated with the vegetable oil. In a large sauce pan over medium heat, add the broccoli and 1 teaspoon salt. Cover the broccoli with water. Bring the broccoli to a boil and cook for 2 minutes. Remove the pan from the heat and drain all the water from the broccoli. Rinse the broccoli with cold water and drain all the water again.

Add the broccoli to the macaroni in the bowl. In a large sauce pan over medium heat, add the spinach, butter, 1/2 teaspoon salt, onion and mushrooms. Saute the vegetables for 4 minutes. Sprinkle the all purpose flour over the mushrooms. Stir constantly and cook for 1 minute. Keep stirring and add the whole milk. Stir frequently and cook about 6-8 minutes or until the sauce is thick and bubbly.

Remove the pan from the heat and add 1 1/2 cups cheddar cheese, whipping cream, black pepper and nutmeg. Stir until well combined and add to the macaroni. Stir until combined.

Preheat the oven to 375°. Spray a 9 x 13 casserole dish with non stick cooking spray. Spoon the noodle filling into the casserole dish. Sprinkle 1/2 cup cheddar cheese over the top. Bake for 40 minutes or until the casserole is hot and bubbly. Remove the dish from the oven and serve.

Blue Cheese Macaroni Bake

Makes 6 servings

Ingredients

2 quarts water
1 tsp. salt
8 oz. pkg. elbow macaroni
1/4 cup unsalted butter
1/4 cup all purpose flour
2 cups whole milk
4 oz. pkg. crumbled blue cheese
1 egg, beaten
2 oz. jar red pimentos, drained
1/2 cup soft breadcrumbs
1/2 cup finely chopped walnuts

Directions

In a large sauce pan over medium heat, add 2 quarts water and salt. Bring the water to a boil and add the elbow macaroni. Boil for 6-7 minutes or until the macaroni is tender. Remove the pan from the heat and drain all the water from the macaroni.

In a large skillet over medium heat, add the butter. When the butter melts, add the all purpose flour. Stir constantly and cook for 1 minute. Keep stirring and slowly add the milk. Stir constantly until the sauce thickens and bubbles. Add the blue cheese and stir until the cheese melts. Remove the skillet from the heat.

Add the egg to a small bowl. Add 1/4 cup cheese sauce to the egg. Whisk until well combined. Add the egg to the cheese sauce and whisk until well combined. Spray a 2 quart casserole dish with non stick cooking spray. Preheat the oven to 350°. Spoon the macaroni, red pimentos and cheese sauce into the casserole dish. Stir until combined.

Sprinkle the breadcrumbs and walnuts over the top of the casserole. Bake for 30 minutes or until the casserole is hot and bubbly. Remove the dish from the oven and cool for 5 minutes before serving.

Monterey Jack Macaroni Bake

Makes 6 servings

Ingredients

2 quarts water
1 tsp. salt
8 oz. pkg. elbow macaroni
2 tbs. unsalted butter
1/4 cup chopped onion
1/4 cup chopped red bell pepper
2 cups shredded Monterey Jack cheese
10.75 oz. can cream of celery soup
1/2 cup sour cream
1/4 tsp. chili powder

Directions

In a large sauce pan over medium heat, add 2 quarts water and salt. Bring the water to a boil and add the elbow macaroni. Boil for 6-7 minutes or until the macaroni is tender. Remove the pan from the heat and drain all the water from the macaroni.

In a large skillet over medium heat, add the butter. When the butter is hot and sizzling, add the onion and red bell pepper. Saute the vegetables for 4 minutes. Remove the skillet from the heat and add the Monterey Jack cheese, cream of celery soup and sour cream. Stir until well combined.

Preheat the oven to 350°. Spray a 2 quart casserole dish with non stick cooking spray. Add the macaroni and cheese sauce to the casserole dish. Stir until well combined. Sprinkle the chili powder over the top of the casserole. Bake for 30 minutes or until the casserole is hot and bubbly. Remove the casserole from the heat and serve.

You can add 2 cups cooked ham, chicken, turkey or leftover roast to the casserole if desired.

Turkey Picante Noodle Casserole

Makes 6 servings

Ingredients

8 oz. egg noodles
2 eggs, beaten
1 cup whipping cream
8 oz. container plain yogurt
1 cup shredded Monterey Jack cheese
1 tbs. dried Italian seasoning
1 1/2 cups picante sauce
1 lb. cooked chopped turkey
1/2 cup grated Parmesan cheese

Directions

In a large sauce pan over medium heat, add 2 quarts water. Bring the water to a boil and add the egg noodles. Boil for 6-7 minutes or until the noodles are tender. Remove the pan from the heat and drain all the water from the noodles.

In a mixing bowl, add the eggs, whipping cream, yogurt, Monterey Jack cheese and Italian seasoning. Stir until well mixed. Preheat the oven to 350°. Spray a 9 x 13 baking dish with non stick cooking spray.

Place half the noodles in the bottom of the baking dish. Spoon 3/4 cup picante sauce over the noodles. Spread half the turkey over the sauce. Spread half the cheese sauce over the turkey. Repeat the layering process one more time.

Sprinkle the Parmesan cheese over the top. Cover the dish with aluminum foil or a lid. Bake for 30 minutes or until the casserole is hot and bubbly. Remove the aluminum foil and bake for 5 minutes or until the Parmesan cheese is lightly browned. Remove the dish from the oven and cool for 5 minutes before serving.

Plentiful Pasta & Black Eye Pea Salad

Makes 8 servings

Ingredients

4 cups cooked black eye peas
2 cups cooked rotelle pasta
1 red bell pepper, chopped
1 green bell pepper, chopped
1 purple onion, chopped
6 oz. provolone cheese, cubed
3 oz. sliced pepperoni, cut into thin strips
2 oz. jar diced pimento, drained
4 oz. jar sliced mushrooms, drained
2 tbs. minced fresh parsley
1 envelope dry Italian salad dressing mix
1/4 tsp. black pepper
1/4 cup granulated sugar
1/2 cup vinegar
1/4 cup vegetable oil

Directions

In a large bowl, add the black eye peas, pasta, red bell pepper, green bell pepper, onion, provolone cheese, pepperoni, pimento, mushrooms and parsley.

In a jar with a lid, add the dry Italian dressing mix, black pepper, granulated sugar, vinegar and vegetable oil. Place the lid on the jar and shake until well combined. Pour the dressing over the salad.

Toss until well combined. Cover the bowl and chill at least 2 hours before serving.

Garden Macaroni Salad

Makes 8 servings

Ingredients

8 oz. pkg. elbow macaroni
1 cup diced cucumber
1 cup sliced celery
1/4 cup chopped green bell pepper
1/4 cup sliced radishes
2 tsp. chopped green onions
2 tomatoes, diced
3/4 cup mayonnaise
1 tsp. salt
1/4 tsp. dried basil

Directions

In a large sauce pan over medium heat, add 8 cups water. Bring the water to a boil and add the macaroni. Boil for 6-7 minutes or until the macaroni is tender. Remove the pan from the heat and drain all the water from the macaroni. Rinse the macaroni in cold water and drain all the water again.

Add the macaroni, cucumber, celery, green bell pepper, radishes, green onions, tomatoes, mayonnaise, salt and basil to a serving bowl. Stir until well combined. Cover the bowl and chill at least 3 hours before serving.

Asparagus Pasta Salad

Makes 12 servings

Ingredients

1 lb. fresh asparagus, cut into 1 1/2" pieces
1 lb. corkscrew pasta, cooked
1 cup diced cooked chicken
1 cup diced cooked ham
2 tomatoes, peeled and diced
1/2 cup sliced black olives
1 1/2 cups prepared Italian dressing
1 1/2 tsp. fresh dill, minced

Directions

In a sauce pan over medium heat, add the asparagus. Cover the asparagus with water and bring to a boil. Cook for 4 minutes or until the asparagus is crisp tender. Remove the pan from the heat and drain all the water from the asparagus. Rinse the asparagus in cold water and drain all the water again.

Add the asparagus, pasta, chicken, ham, tomatoes, black olives, Italian dressing and dill to a large serving bowl. Toss until well combined. Cover the bowl and chill the salad for 4 hours before serving.

Garden Tortellini Salad

Makes 12 servings

Ingredients

9 oz. pkg. refrigerated cheese filled tortellini
7 oz. pkg. refrigerated cheese filled spinach tortellini
3 cups fresh broccoli florets
2 cups carrots, thinly sliced
1 red bell pepper, cut into thin strips
2 green onions, sliced
1/4 cup fresh chopped basil
1 tbs. lemon juice
1 1/2 tsp. Dijon mustard
1 1/2 tsp. balsamic vinegar
1 1/2 tsp. grated orange zest
1/2 tsp. dried thyme
1/2 tsp. salt
1/8 tsp. black pepper
1/2 cup vegetable oil
1/4 cup olive oil

Directions

In a large sauce pan over medium heat, add 12 cups water. Bring the water to a boil and add both packages of tortellini. Boil for 3-5 minutes or until the tortellini is tender. Remove the pan from the heat and drain all the water from the tortellini. Rinse the tortellini with cold water and drain all the water from the pasta again.

In a sauce pan over medium heat, add the broccoli and carrots. Cover the vegetables with water and bring to a boil. Cook for 5 minutes or until the vegetables are tender. Remove the pan from the heat and drain all the water from the pan. Rinse the vegetables in cold water and drain all the water again from the pan.

Add the tortellini, broccoli, carrots, red bell pepper, green onions and basil to a large bowl. In a food processor, add the lemon juice, Dijon mustard, balsamic vinegar, orange zest, thyme, salt and black pepper. Process until combined. With the food processor running, slowly add the vegetable and olive oil. Process until smooth and combined. Pour the dressing over the tortellini and vegetables. Toss until combined. Cover the bowl and chill for 2 hours before serving.

Southwestern Pasta Salad

Makes 8 servings

Ingredients

1 cup sour cream
16 oz. jar thick and chunky mild salsa
1/2 tsp. ground cumin
2 garlic cloves, minced
1 lb. penne pasta
15 oz. can black beans, rinsed and drained
8 oz. can whole kernel corn, drained
1 red bell pepper, chopped
3 green onions, sliced
1/4 cup chopped fresh cilantro

Directions

In a mixing bowl, add the sour cream, salsa, cumin and garlic. Stir until well combined. Cover the bowl and chill for 1 hour.

In a large sauce pan over medium heat, add 2 quarts water. Bring the water to a boil and add the penne pasta. Boil for 7-8 minutes or until the pasta is tender. Remove the pan from the heat and drain all the water from the pasta. Rinse the pasta with cold water and drain all the water from the pasta again.

In a large bowl, add the penne pasta, chilled sour cream dressing, black beans, corn, red bell pepper, green onions and cilantro. Toss until well combined. Cover the bowl and chill for 2 hours before serving.

Tossed Shell Salad

Makes 8 servings

Ingredients

2 3/4 cups small shell pasta
1 cup cherry tomatoes, halved
1 cup shredded cheddar cheese
1/2 cup sliced green onions
1 green bell pepper, thinly sliced
1/4 cup vegetable oil
2 tbs. lemon juice
2 tbs. white wine vinegar
1 tsp. dried dill
1 tsp. dried oregano
1/2 tsp. salt
1/8 tsp. black pepper

Directions

In a large sauce pan over medium heat, add 10 cups water. Bring the water to a boil and add the shell pasta. Boil for 6-7 minutes or until the pasta shells are tender. Remove the pan from the heat and drain all the water from the pasta. Rinse the pasta with cold water and drain all the water again from the pasta.

Add the pasta, tomatoes, cheddar cheese, green onions and green bell pepper to a mixing bowl. In a small bowl, add the vegetable oil, lemon juice, white wine vinegar, dill, oregano, salt and black pepper. Whisk until well combined. Pour the dressing over the pasta and vegetables. Toss until blended. Cover the bowl and chill for 2 hours before serving.

Cabbage Slaw Pasta Salad

Do not knock this salad until you try it. It is a cross between slaw and a pasta salad.

Makes 4 servings

Ingredients

4 oz. small shell macaroni
2 hard boiled eggs, chopped
1/2 cup shredded cabbage
1/4 cup chopped green bell pepper
1/4 cup chopped celery
1/4 cup mayonnaise
1 tbs. minced sweet pickle
1 tbs. Thousand Island dressing
1/4 tsp. salt
1.8 tsp. black pepper

Directions

In a large sauce pan over medium heat, add 8 cups water. Bring the water to a boil and add the macaroni. Boil for 6-7 minutes or until the macaroni is tender. Remove the pan from the heat and drain all the water from the macaroni. Rinse the macaroni with cold water and drain all the water from the macaroni again.

In a large bowl, add the macaroni, eggs, cabbage, green bell pepper, celery, mayonnaise, sweet pickle, Thousand Island dressing, salt and black pepper. Toss until well combined. Cover the bowl and chill for 2 hours before serving.

Confetti Orzo Pasta Salad

Makes 8 servings

Ingredients

1 1/2 cups dry orzo pasta
1 carrot, chopped
1 1/4 cups green bell pepper
1/2 cup peeled, seeded and chopped cucumber
1/4 cup thinly sliced green onions
1/4 cup chopped purple onion
1/4 cup chopped fresh parsley
1/2 tsp. grated lemon zest
3 tbs. lemon juice
2 tbs. white wine vinegar
3/4 tsp. salt
1/8 tsp. black pepper
2 garlic cloves, minced
1/3 cup olive oil

Directions

In a large sauce pan over medium heat, add 8 cups water. Bring the water to a boil and add the orzo. Boil for 5 minutes or until the orzo is tender. Remove the pan from the heat and drain all the water from the pasta. Rinse the pasta with cold water and drain all the water from the pasta again.

In a large bowl, add the orzo, carrot, green bell pepper, cucumber, green onions, purple onion and parsley. Toss until combined. In a small bowl, add the lemon zest, lemon juice, white wine vinegar, salt, black pepper and garlic. Whisk until blended. While constantly whisking, slowly add the olive oil. Whisk until the dressing is well blended and slightly thickened.

Pour the dressing over the orzo and vegetables. Toss until blended. Cover the bowl and chill for 2 hours before serving.

Linguine Vegetable Pasta Salad

Makes 8 servings

Ingredients

1 lb. pkg. linguine noodles, broken into thirds
6 cups shredded red cabbage
4 carrots, shredded
3 tomatoes, finely chopped
3 celery stalks, finely chopped
1 large purple onion, chopped
1 large green bell pepper, chopped
8 oz. bottle Italian salad dressing
1 1/2 tbs. Mrs. Dash seasoning blend

Directions

In a large sauce pan over medium heat, add 12 cups water. Bring the water to a boil and add the linguine noodles. Boil for 6-7 minutes or until the noodles are tender. Remove the pan from the heat and drain all the water from the noodles. Rinse the noodles with cold water and drain all the water again.

In a large bowl, add the linguine, cabbage, carrots, tomatoes, celery, purple onion, green bell pepper, Italian salad dressing and Mrs. Dash seasoning. Toss until well combined. Cover the bowl and chill for 4 hours before serving. Toss the salad again before serving.

Broccoli Cauliflower Pasta Salad

Makes 6 servings

Ingredients

4 oz. spaghetti noodles
2 cups chopped cauliflower florets
2 cups chopped broccoli florets
1 onion, sliced and separated into rings
2 cups sliced fresh mushrooms
1/2 cup red bell pepper, cut into strips
1/2 cup green bell pepper, cut into strips
1/2 cup yellow bell pepper, cut into strips
1/4 cup sliced black olives
1/4 cup mayonnaise
3 tbs. vegetable oil
3 tbs. apple cider vinegar
2 tbs. granulated sugar
1 tsp. black pepper
1 tsp. paprika
1/2 tsp. salt

Directions

Break the spaghetti noodles in half. In a large sauce pan over medium heat, add 8 cups water. Bring the water to a boil and add the spaghetti noodles. Boil for 6-7 minutes or until the noodles are tender. Remove the pan from the heat and drain all the water from the noodles. Rinse the noodles with cold water and drain again.

Add the noodles, cauliflower, broccoli, onion, mushrooms, red bell pepper, green bell pepper, yellow bell pepper and olives to a large bowl. Toss until combined.

In a small bowl, add the mayonnaise, vegetable oil, apple cider vinegar, granulated sugar, black pepper, paprika and salt. Whisk until well combined and add to the noodles and vegetables. Toss until combined. Cover the bowl and chill for 3 hours before serving.

Pistachio Pasta Salad

Makes 6 servings

Ingredients

1 3/4 cups rotini pasta
1/4 cup red wine vinegar
1/4 cup olive oil
3/4 tsp. dried oregano
1/8 tsp. garlic powder
1/8 tsp. black pepper
1 cup fresh snow peas
2 cups torn fresh spinach
1 cup chopped fresh tomato
1/3 cup chopped pistachios
1 tbs. grated Parmesan cheese

Directions

In a large sauce pan over medium heat, add 8 cups water. Bring the water to a boil and add the pasta. Boil for 8 minutes or until the pasta is tender. Remove the pan from the heat and drain all the water from the pasta.

While the pasta is cooking, make the dressing. In a jar with a lid, add the red wine vinegar, olive oil, oregano, garlic powder and black pepper. Place the lid on the jar and shake until well combined. Pour the dressing over the hot cooked pasta. Gently toss until combined. Set the pasta aside to cool at room temperature.

Add the cooled pasta, snow peas, spinach and tomato to a serving bowl. Toss until combined. Sprinkle the pistachios and Parmesan cheese over the top of the pasta. Cover the bowl and chill for 2 hours before serving.

Macaroni and Cheese Salad

Makes 8 servings

Ingredients

1 1/2 cups elbow macaroni
2 tbs. vegetable oil
1/2 cup mayonnaise
1 tbs. granulated sugar
1/2 tsp. salt
1/4 tsp. black pepper
1/2 cup diced cooked ham
1 cup shredded cheddar cheese
1/4 cup sliced green onions
1/2 cup frozen green peas, thawed

Directions

In a large sauce pan over medium heat, add 8 cups water. Bring the water to a boil and add the macaroni. Boil for 6-7 minutes or until the macaroni is tender. Remove the pan from the heat and drain all the water from the macaroni. Rinse the macaroni with cold water and drain all the water again.

Add the macaroni and vegetable oil to a large bowl. Toss until the macaroni is coated with the oil. Add the mayonnaise, granulated sugar, salt, black pepper, ham, cheddar cheese, green onions and green peas. Toss until combined. Cover the bowl and chill for 2 hours before serving.

Pasta Bean Salad

Makes 4 servings

Ingredients

1/2 cup mayonnaise
1/4 cup chopped fresh parsley
1/4 cup grated Parmesan cheese
2 tbs. lemon juice
1 garlic clove, finely minced
1 tsp. dried basil
2 cups cooked elbow macaroni
15 oz. can kidney beans, rinsed and drained
1 cup frozen green peas, thawed
1 cup diced carrots

Directions

In a small bowl, add the mayonnaise, parsley, Parmesan cheese, lemon juice, garlic and basil. Stir until well combined. In a serving bowl, add the macaroni, kidney beans, green peas and carrots. Add the mayonnaise dressing to the macaroni and beans. Stir until combined. Cover the bowl and chill for 2 hours before serving.

Pasta Basil Toss

Makes 6 servings

Ingredients

1 cup broccoli florets
1 cup cauliflower florets
1 cup fresh snow peas
2 garlic cloves, minced
3 tbs. chopped fresh basil
1 tbs. unsalted butter
3 cups small shaped pasta, cooked
1/3 cup grated Parmesan cheese
2 oz. jar diced red pimento, drained
Salt and black pepper to taste

Directions

In a large sauce pan over medium heat, add the broccoli and cauliflower. Cover the vegetables with water and bring the water to a boil. Cook for 3 minutes. Add the snow peas and cook for 1 minute. Remove the pan from the heat and drain all the water from the vegetables. Rinse the vegetables with cold water to stop the cooking process.

In a sauce pan over medium heat, add the garlic, basil and butter. Saute the garlic for 4 minutes or until the garlic is tender. Remove the pan from the heat and spoon into a serving bowl. Add the vegetables, pasta, Parmesan cheese and red pimento to the bowl. Toss until combined. Season to taste with salt and black pepper. Serve the salad at room temperature.

Caesar Presto Pasta Salad

Makes 10 servings

Ingredients

16 oz. pkg. fusilli pasta
1 red bell pepper, cut into thin strips
1 cup sliced fresh mushrooms
1 cup broccoli florets
12 oz. bottle Caesar salad dressing

Directions

In a large sauce pan over medium heat, add 12 cups water. Bring the water to a boil and add the pasta. Boil for 8-10 minutes or until the pasta is tender. Remove the pan from the heat and drain all the water from the pasta. Rinse the pasta with cold water and drain all the water from the pasta again.

Add the pasta, red bell pepper, mushrooms, broccoli and Caesar dressing to a large bowl. Toss until well combined. You can serve the salad at room temperature or chilled. Toss the salad again before serving if chilled.

Caesar Ravioli Salad

Makes 4 servings

Ingredients

9 oz. pkg. refrigerated cheese ravioli
2 cups cherry tomato halves
1 cucumber, thinly sliced
1/2 cup chopped purple onion
1/4 cup sliced black olives
1/4 cup freshly grated Parmesan cheese
1/2 tsp. black pepper
3/4 cup prepared Caesar salad dressing
4 cups shredded romaine lettuce

Directions

In a large sauce pan over medium heat, add 2 quarts water. Bring the water to a boil and add the ravioli. Boil for 6-7 minutes or until the ravioli is tender. Remove the pan from the heat and drain all the water from the ravioli. Rinse the ravioli with cold water and drain all the water again.

Add the ravioli to a large bowl. Add the cherry tomatoes, cucumber, purple onion, black olives, Parmesan cheese, black pepper and Caesar dressing. Toss until well blended. Cover the bowl and chill for 2 hours before serving.

When ready to serve, place the lettuce on serving plates. Spoon the ravioli salad over the lettuce.

Green Bean Pasta Salad

Makes 4 servings

Ingredients

1 cup shell macaroni
1 cup fresh green beans, cut into 1" pieces
1/4 tsp. salt
1 cup cherry tomato halves
1/4 cup diced cucumber
1/4 cup prepared Italian salad dressing
1/4 cup sliced radishes

Directions

In a large sauce pan over medium heat, add 8 cups water. Bring the water to a boil and add the macaroni, green beans and salt. Boil for 6-7 minutes or until the macaroni is tender. Remove the pan from the heat and drain all the water from the pan. Rinse the macaroni and green beans in cold water and drain all the water again. Cool the macaroni and green beans for 15 minutes at room temperature.

In a serving bowl, add the macaroni and green beans, tomatoes, cucumber and Italian salad dressing. Toss until well combined. Cover the bowl and chill for 2 hours. Gently stir in the radishes and serve.

Vegetable Pasta Salad

Makes 12 servings

Ingredients

1/4 cup olive oil
1 tsp. dried thyme
1/2 tsp. dried oregano
2 garlic cloves, minced
1/2 tsp. dried savory
1/2 tsp. dried basil
3/4 tsp. salt
2 cups chopped onion
3/4 tsp. black pepper
12 oz. pkg. corkscrew macaroni
1/2 cup sliced celery
1/2 cup sliced green onions
2 cups green bell pepper, cut into thin strips
2 tomatoes, cut into wedges
1/2 cup green olives
1/2 cup black olives, halved
1/4 cup lemon juice

Directions

In a sauce pan over medium heat, add the olive oil. When the oil is hot, remove the pan from the heat. Add the thyme, oregano, garlic, savory, basil, 1/2 teaspoon salt, onion and 1/2 teaspoon black pepper to the pan. Stir until combined. Let the seasonings and onion sit at room temperature for 1 hour.

In a large sauce pan over medium heat, add 10 cups water. Bring the water to a boil and add the macaroni. Boil for 8-10 minutes or until the macaroni is tender. Remove the pan from the heat and drain all the water from the pasta. Rinse the pasta with cold water and drain all the water from the pasta again.

Add the oil and seasonings from the sauce pan to a large bowl. Add the pasta, celery, green onions, green bell peppers, tomatoes, green olives, black olives, lemon juice, 1/4 teaspoon salt and 1/4 teaspoon black pepper. Toss until well combined. Cover the bowl and chill for 8 hours before serving.

Oriental Pasta Salad

Makes 8 servings

Ingredients

8 oz. linguine pasta, broken into pieces
1/2 cup vegetable oil
1/2 cup soy sauce
1 garlic clove, minced
1/4 cup lemon juice
1/4 tsp. Tabasco sauce
2 tbs. sesame seeds, toasted
4 green onions, sliced
2 carrots, thinly sliced
12 cherry tomatoes, halved
3 cups broccoli florets, chopped

Directions

In a large sauce pan over medium heat, add 8 cups water. Bring the water to a boil and add the pasta. Boil for 6-7 minutes or until the pasta is tender. Remove the pan from the heat and drain all the water from the pasta. Rinse the pasta with cold water and drain all the water again.

In a jar with a lid, add the vegetable oil, soy sauce, garlic, lemon juice, Tabasco sauce and sesame seeds. Place the lid on the jar and toss until combined.

In a large bowl, add the linguine, dressing, green onions, carrots, tomatoes and broccoli. Toss until well combined. Serve the salad at room temperature.

Ratatouille Pasta Salad

Makes 8 servings

Ingredients

8 oz. rotini pasta
1 large eggplant
1/2 tsp. salt
1/2 cup chopped onion
1 tsp. minced garlic
2 zucchini, sliced
1/2 cup green bell pepper, cut into 1" strips
1/2 cup red bell pepper, cut into 1" strips
1/4 cup olive oil
1/4 tsp. black pepper
1/2 cup chopped fresh basil
1 tbs. chopped fresh parsley
3 tbs. lemon juice

Directions

In a large sauce pan over medium heat, add 8 cups water. Bring the water to a boil and add the pasta. Boil for 8-10 minutes or until the pasta is tender. Remove the pan from the heat and drain all the water from the pasta. Rinse the pasta with cold water and drain all the water again.

Peel the eggplant and cut the eggplant into 3/4" cubes. Sprinkle the salt over the eggplant. Preheat the oven to 400°. Add the eggplant to a roasting pan. Cover the eggplant with aluminum foil or a lid. Bake for 25 minutes or until the eggplant is tender. Remove from the oven and remove the aluminum foil. Let the eggplant cool while you prepare the rest of the salad.

In a large skillet over medium heat, add the onion, garlic, zucchini, green bell pepper, red bell pepper and 2 tablespoons olive oil. Saute the vegetables until they are crisp tender or about 4 minutes. Add the pasta, remaining olive oil, black pepper, basil, parsley and lemon juice. Toss until combined and remove the skillet from the heat.

Spoon the salad into a serving bowl. Add the eggplant and toss until combined. Cover the bowl and chill for 1 hour before serving.

Vinaigrette Pasta Vegetable Salad

Makes 12 servings

Ingredients

1/3 cup plus 2 tbs. olive oil
1/4 cup red wine vinegar
1 tbs. water
1 tsp. minced onion
1/4 tsp. granulated sugar
1/4 tsp. paprika
1/4 tsp. black pepper
1/8 tsp. dry mustard
2 garlic cloves, minced
1 1/4 tsp. salt
8 oz. pkg. corkscrew macaroni
1 onion, chopped
1 cup sliced fresh mushrooms
1 carrot, thinly sliced
1 cup broccoli florets
1 zucchini, thinly sliced
2 tsp. dried basil
1 cup frozen green peas, thawed
1 pint cherry tomatoes, cut in half
2 tbs. chopped fresh parsley

Directions

In a jar with a lid, add 1/3 cup olive oil, red wine vinegar, water, minced onion, granulated sugar, paprika, black pepper, dry mustard,

1 garlic clove and 1/4 teaspoon salt. Place the lid on the jar and shake until well combined.

In a large sauce pan over medium heat, add 10 cups water. Bring the water to a boil and add the macaroni and 1 teaspoon salt. Boil for 8-10 minutes or until the macaroni is tender. Remove the pan from the heat and drain all the water from the pasta. Rinse the pasta with cold water and drain all the water from the pasta again.

In a skillet over medium heat, add the onion, mushrooms, 1 garlic clove and 2 tablespoons olive oil. Saute for 4 minutes or until the onion and mushrooms are tender. Add the carrot, broccoli, zucchini, basil and green peas. Saute the vegetables for 3 minutes. Remove from the heat and add to a large bowl.

Add the macaroni and dressing to the bowl. Toss until well combined. Add the tomatoes and parsley. Toss the salad again. You can serve the salad at room temperature or chilled.

Water Chestnut Pasta Salad

Makes 12 servings

Ingredients

1 lb. rotini pasta
3/4 cup vegetable oil
1/4 cup cider vinegar
1 1/2 tsp. salt
1 1/2 tsp. black pepper
1 garlic clove, crushed
1 green bell pepper, chopped
1 red bell pepper, chopped
8 oz. can sliced water chestnuts, drained
6 green onions, chopped
1 cup cherry tomatoes, halved

Directions

In a large sauce pan over medium heat, add 12 cups water. Bring the water to a boil and add the pasta. Boil for 6-7 minutes or until the pasta is tender. Remove the pan from the heat and drain all the water from the pasta. Rinse the pasta with cold water and drain all the water again.

In a jar with a lid, add the vegetable oil, cider vinegar, salt, black pepper and garlic. Place the lid on the jar and shake until the dressing is combined. In a large serving bowl, add the pasta, green bell pepper, red bell pepper, water chestnuts, green onions, tomatoes and dressing. Toss until well combined.

Cover the bowl and chill for 8 hours before serving. Toss the salad again before serving.

Garden Pasta Medley

Makes 6 servings

Ingredients

8 oz. pkg. small shell macaroni
1 cup broccoli florets
3/4 cup thinly sliced yellow squash
1/2 cup chopped red bell pepper
1/2 cup thinly sliced radishes
1/4 cup chopped celery
2 tbs. fresh chopped parsley
4 oz. cheddar cheese, cubed
8 oz. bottle creamy cucumber salad dressing

Directions

In a large sauce pan over medium heat, add 8 cups water. Bring the water to a boil and add the macaroni. Boil for 6-7 minutes or until the macaroni is tender. Remove the pan from the heat and drain all the water from the macaroni. Rinse the macaroni with cold water and drain all the water again.

In a large bowl, add the macaroni, broccoli, squash, red bell pepper, radishes, celery, parsley, cheddar cheese and cucumber dressing. Toss until well combined. Cover the bowl and chill the salad for 2 hours before serving.

Artichoke Salami Pasta Salad

Makes 6 servings

Ingredients

4 oz. dry spaghetti, broken into pieces
3/4 cup sliced fresh zucchini
2/3 cup shredded carrots
2 oz. salami, cut into thin strips
1 cup shredded mozzarella cheese
2 tbs. grated Parmesan cheese
6 oz. jar marinated artichokes
2 tbs. vegetable oil
2 tbs. vinegar
3/4 tsp. dry mustard
1/2 tsp. dried oregano
1/2 tsp. dried basil
1 garlic clove, crushed

Directions

In a large sauce pan over medium heat, add 8 cups water. Bring the water to a boil and add the spaghetti. Boil for 6-7 minutes or until the spaghetti is tender. Remove the pan from the heat and drain all the water from the spaghetti. Rinse the spaghetti in cold water and drain all the water again.

Add the spaghetti to a serving bowl. Add the zucchini, carrots, salami, mozzarella cheese and Parmesan cheese. Drain the artichokes and save the artichoke liquid in a jar with a lid. Add the artichokes to the serving bowl. Add the vegetable oil, vinegar, dry mustard, oregano, basil and garlic to the jar. Place the lid on the jar and shake until well combined. Shake at least 1 minute. Pour the dressing over the salad and toss until well combined.

Cover the bowl and chill for 3 hours before serving.

Deli Style Macaroni Salad

Makes 6 servings

Ingredients

8 oz. small shell macaroni
1 cup chopped celery
1/4 cup chopped green bell pepper
1/4 cup chopped red bell pepper
1/4 cup chopped purple onion
1/2 cup mayonnaise
1/2 cup sour cream
1/4 cup half and half
1/2 tsp. salt
1/4 tsp. black pepper

Directions

In a large sauce pan over medium heat, add 8 cups water. Bring the water to a boil and add the macaroni. Boil for 6-7 minutes or until the macaroni is tender. Remove the pan from the heat and drain all the water from the macaroni. Rinse the macaroni in cold water and drain all the water again.

Add the macaroni, celery, green bell pepper, red bell pepper and purple onion to a serving bowl. In a small bowl, add the mayonnaise, sour cream, half and half, salt and black pepper. Whisk until smooth. Add the dressing to the macaroni and vegetables. Toss until well combined.

Cover the bowl and refrigerate for 2 hours before serving.

Dilled Macaroni Salad

Makes 6 servings

Ingredients

1 cup elbow macaroni
1/2 cup chopped onion
1/4 cup chopped celery
1/4 cup chopped green bell pepper
1/4 cup shredded carrot
1/2 cup mayonnaise
1 tbs. vinegar
1 tsp. dried dill
1/4 tsp. garlic salt
1/4 tsp. onion salt

Directions

In a large sauce pan over medium heat, add 8 cups water. Bring the water to a boil and add the macaroni. Boil for 6-7 minutes or until the macaroni is tender. Remove the pan from the heat and drain all the water from the macaroni. Rinse the macaroni with cold water and drain all the water again.

In a large bowl, add the macaroni, onion, celery, green bell pepper, carrot, mayonnaise, vinegar, dill, garlic salt and onion salt. Stir until well combined. Cover the bowl and chill for 2 hours before serving.

Tomato Olive Pasta Salad

Makes 6 servings

Ingredients

4 tomatoes, peeled and chopped
1/4 cup green olives, sliced
1 garlic clove, minced
1/2 tsp. dried oregano
1 1/2 tbs. minced fresh parsley
1/4 tsp. salt
1/8 tsp. black pepper
1/4 cup olive oil
1 tbs. olive juice
6 oz. fettuccine noodles, cooked

Directions

In a serving bowl, add the tomatoes, green olives, garlic, oregano, parsley, salt, black pepper, olive oil and olive juice. Stir until combined. Let the salad sit for 30 minutes at room temperature. Add the fettuccine and toss until well combined. Cover the bowl and refrigerate for 2 hours before serving.

Spinach Dijon Pasta Salad

Makes 12 servings

Ingredients

1 lb. pkg. corkscrew pasta
8 oz. fresh spinach
1/4 cup Dijon mustard
2 tbs. olive oil
1 garlic clove, minced
1/2 tsp. salt
1/4 tsp. black pepper
1 tsp. dried basil
1/4 cup chopped walnuts
1 cup ricotta cheese
1 tbs. lemon juice

Directions

In a large sauce pan over medium heat, add 8 cups water. Bring the water to a boil and add the pasta. Boil for 6-7 minutes or until the pasta is tender. Remove the pan from the heat and drain all the water from the pasta. Rinse the pasta in cold water and drain all the water again.

Remove the stems from the spinach if needed. In a food processor, add the Dijon mustard, olive oil, garlic, salt, black pepper, basil and walnuts. Process until smooth. Add the ricotta cheese, lemon juice and spinach. Process until smooth. Depending upon your food processor, you may need to add the spinach in 1 cup increments. Use all the spinach and process until smooth.

Add the pasta to a serving bowl. Pour the spinach sauce over the pasta. Toss until well combined. Cover the bowl and refrigerate for 2 hours before serving.

Artichoke Hearts Pasta

Makes 6 servings

Ingredients

16 oz. jar artichoke hearts, drained and quartered
2/3 cup sliced black olives
1/4 cup olive oil
3 tbs. lemon juice
2 garlic cloves, minced
3 dashes Tabasco sauce
1/2 tsp. salt
1/4 tsp. black pepper
8 oz. linguine noodles, cooked

Directions

In a serving bowl, add the artichoke hearts, black olives, olive oil, lemon juice, garlic, Tabasco sauce, salt and black pepper. Stir until combined. Let the salad sit at room temperature for 1 hour.

Add the linguine noodles and toss until well combined. Cover the bowl and chill for 2 hours before serving.

Ramen Noodle Salad

Makes 4 servings

Ingredients

4 cups water
2 pkgs. chicken flavored ramen noodles, 3 oz. size
2 tsp. unsalted butter
1/2 cup finely chopped celery
1/2 cup shredded carrots
1/2 cup thinly sliced green onions
2 tbs. finely chopped green bell pepper
2 tsp. lemon juice
2 tsp. soy sauce
4 tbs. mayonnaise

Directions

In a sauce pan over medium heat, add the water. When the water boils, add the ramen noodles and seasoning packet. Stir until the seasoning dissolves. Bring the water to a boil and cook for 2 minutes. Stir frequently so the noodles separate. Remove the pan from the heat and drain all the water from the noodles. Add the butter and toss until the butter melts.

Add the noodles to a serving bowl. Add the celery, carrots, green onions, green bell pepper, lemon juice, soy sauce and mayonnaise. Stir until well combined. Cover the bowl and chill for 3 hours before serving.

Gourmet Macaroni Salad

Makes 8 servings

Ingredients

8 oz. pkg. elbow macaroni
16 oz. can peas and carrots, drained
1 cup chopped dill pickles
1 cup chopped celery
2 tbs. dried minced onion
1 tbs. yellow prepared mustard
1 1/2 tsp. lemon pepper seasoning
1/8 tsp. anchovy paste
1/2 tsp. salt
1/2 cup mayonnaise
1/2 cup cherry tomatoes

Directions

In a large sauce pan over medium heat, add 8 cups water. Bring the water to a boil and add the macaroni. Boil for 6-7 minutes or until the macaroni is tender. Remove the pan from the heat and drain all the water from the macaroni. Rinse the macaroni with cold water and drain all the water again.

In a serving bowl, add the macaroni, peas and carrots, dill pickles, celery, onion, mustard, lemon pepper seasoning, anchovy paste, salt and mayonnaise. Stir until well blended. Cover the bowl and chill for 2 hours. Place the cherry tomatoes on top of the salad before serving.

Parmesan Artichoke Salad

Makes 4 servings

Ingredients

3 cups cooked rotini pasta
1/2 cup Italian salad dressing
3/4 cup red bell pepper, cut into strips
1/2 cup thinly sliced carrot
1/4 cup sliced green onions
14 oz. can artichoke hearts, drained and diced
1/2 cup grated Parmesan cheese
1/4 tsp. dried basil
1/4 tsp. black pepper

Directions

Add all the ingredients to a serving bowl. Toss until well combined. Cover the bowl and refrigerate for 2 hours before serving. Stir the pasta salad again before serving.

Tortellini Salad

Makes 8 servings

Ingredients

8 oz. pkg. cheese filled spinach tortellini
1/4 cup olive oil
3 tbs. wine vinegar
1 1/2 tbs. chopped fresh parsley
1 1/2 tsp. dried dill
1/2 tsp. dried oregano
1 1/2 tsp. Dijon mustard
1/4 tsp. salt
1/4 tsp. black pepper
1/2 cup chopped red bell pepper
1/2 cup chopped green bell pepper
1/4 cup chopped green onions
1/4 cup sliced black olives

Directions

In a large sauce pan over medium heat, add 8 cups water. Bring the water to a boil and add the tortellini. Boil for 6-7 minutes or until the tortellini is tender. Remove the pan from the heat and drain all the water from the pasta. Rinse the pasta with cold water and drain all the water again.

In a blender, add the olive oil, wine vinegar, parsley, dill, oregano, mustard, salt and black pepper. Process until smooth. In a serving bowl, add the tortellini, red bell pepper, green bell pepper, green onions and black olives. Pour the dressing over the tortellini. Toss until well combined.

Cover the bowl and chill for 8 hours before serving. Toss the salad again before serving.

Tarragon Vegetable Pasta Salad

Makes 8 servings

Ingredients

1 1/2 cups uncooked elbow macaroni
2 tbs. tarragon vinegar
2 tbs. vegetable oil
1/4 cup mayonnaise
1/2 cup shredded carrot
1/2 cup sliced black olives
3/4 cup diced red bell pepper
1/2 cup fresh snow peas

Directions

In a large sauce pan over medium heat, add 8 cups water. Bring the water to a boil and add the macaroni. Boil for 6-7 minutes or until the macaroni is tender. Remove the pan from the heat and drain all the water from the macaroni. Rinse the macaroni in cold water and drain all the water again. Chill the macaroni for 2 hours.

In a small bowl, whisk together the tarragon vinegar and vegetable oil. Pour the oil and vinegar over the chilled macaroni. Toss until combined. Add the mayonnaise, carrot, black olives, red bell pepper and snow peas. Toss until well combined. Cover the bowl and chill for 3 hours before serving.

Spicy Beef Pasta Salad

Makes 6 servings

Ingredients

1/2 cup soy sauce
1/4 cup Dijon mustard
2 tbs. olive oil
3 tsp. Cajun seasoning
1/2 tsp. red pepper flakes, crushed
1 lb. flank steak
8 oz. pkg. bow tie pasta
1 green bell pepper, chopped
2 cups cherry tomatoes, halved

Directions

In a shallow dish, add the soy sauce, Dijon mustard, olive oil, Cajun seasoning and red pepper flakes. Stir until combined. Remove 1/3 cup marinade and store in a separate bowl. Cover the bowl and chill for 8 hours. Add the flank steak to the rest of the marinade in the dish. Turn the steak over so both sides are coated with the marinade. Cover the dish and marinate at least 8 hours.

Preheat the oven to the broiler position. Remove the steak from the marinade and place on a broiler pan. Discard the marinade from the steak. Broil the steak about 5 minutes on each side or cook the steak to your taste. Remove the steak from the oven and cover the steak with aluminum foil. Let the steak rest for 10 minutes.

While the steak is resting, cook the pasta. In a large sauce pan over medium heat, add 8 cups water. Bring the water to a boil and add the bow tie pasta. Boil for 6-7 minutes or until the pasta is tender.

Remove the pan from the heat and drain all the water from the pasta. Rinse the pasta with cold water and drain all the water from the pasta again.

Slice the steak, against the grain, into thin slices. Add the pasta, steak slices, green bell pepper, tomatoes and 1/3 cup reserved marinade to a large bowl. Toss until combined. You can chill the salad or serve at room temperature.

Chicken Spaghetti Salad

Makes 6 servings

Ingredients

8 oz. spaghetti noodles, broken into pieces
2 cups chopped cooked chicken
2 cup broccoli florets
1 1/2 cups sliced fresh mushrooms
10 cherry tomatoes, halved
1/4 cup chopped purple onion
1/2 cup Italian salad dressing
1 tbs. lemon juice
1 tsp. dried basil
1/2 tsp. season salt
1/2 tsp. Beau Monde seasoning

Directions

In a large sauce pan over medium heat, add 8 cups water. Bring the water to a boil and add the spaghetti. Boil for 6-7 minutes or until the spaghetti noodles are tender. Remove the pan from the heat and drain all the water from the noodles. Rinse the noodles with cold water and drain all the water again.

Add the spaghetti noodles, chicken, broccoli, mushrooms, tomatoes and purple onion to a serving bowl. In a small bowl, stir together the Italian salad dressing, lemon juice, basil, season salt and Beau Monde seasoning. Pour the dressing over the pasta and vegetables. Toss until combined.

Cover the bowl and chill for 2 hours before serving. Toss the salad again before serving.

Dilled Chicken Macaroni Salad

Makes 5 servings

Ingredients

8 oz. pkg. elbow macaroni
1/2 cup evaporated milk
3 tbs. white wine vinegar
2 tbs. chopped green onions
1 tbs. vegetable oil
1 tbs. chopped red pimento
2 tsp. granulated sugar
1 tsp. dried dill
1/2 tsp. salt
1/2 tsp. dry mustard
1/4 tsp. black pepper
1 cup chopped cooked chicken breast

Directions

In a large sauce pan over medium heat, add 8 cups water. Bring the water to a boil and add the macaroni. Boil for 6-7 minutes or until the macaroni is tender. Remove the pan from the heat and drain all the water from the macaroni. Rinse the macaroni with cold water and drain all the water again.

In a jar with a lid, add the evaporated milk, white wine vinegar, green onions, vegetable oil, red pimento, granulated sugar, dill, salt, dry mustard and black pepper. Place the lid on the jar and shake until well combined.

Add the macaroni, chicken and dressing to a large bowl. Toss until well combined. Cover the bowl and chill for 3 hours before serving.

Fruited Pasta Salad

Makes 6 servings

Ingredients

1 1/2 cups rotini pasta
2 cups chopped cooked chicken
1 1/2 cups sliced celery
1 cup seedless green grapes, halved
1/4 cup chopped green bell pepper
1/4 cup chopped purple onion
11 oz. can mandarin oranges, drained
8 oz. can sliced water chestnuts, drained
1/4 cup buttermilk salad dressing
1/4 cup mayonnaise
1 tsp. Beau Monde seasoning
1/4 tsp. salt
1/8 tsp. black pepper

Directions

In a large sauce pan over medium heat, add 8 cups water. Bring the water to a boil and add the rotini pasta. Boil for 6-7 minutes or until the pasta is tender. Remove the pan from the heat and drain all the water from the pasta. Rinse the pasta with cold water and drain all the water from the pasta again.

Add the pasta, chicken, celery, grapes, green bell pepper, onion, mandarin oranges and water chestnuts to a large bowl. In a small bowl, stir together the buttermilk salad dressing, mayonnaise, Beau Monde seasoning, salt and black pepper. Add the dressing to the salad. Stir until well combined. Cover the bowl and chill for 2 hours before serving.

Luncheon Pasta Salad

Makes 4 servings

Ingredients

8 oz. pkg. elbow macaroni
2 cups chopped cooked chicken
11 oz. can mandarin oranges, drained
1/2 cup chopped celery
1/4 tsp. salt
1/4 tsp. black pepper
1/2 cup mayonnaise
1/4 cup blue cheese salad dressing
Lettuce leaves, optional

Directions

In a large sauce pan over medium heat, add 8 cups water. Bring the water to a boil and add the macaroni. Boil for 6-7 minutes or until the macaroni is tender. Remove the pan from the heat and drain all the water from the macaroni. Rinse the macaroni with cold water and drain all the water again.

Add the macaroni, chicken, mandarin oranges, celery, salt, black pepper, mayonnaise and blue cheese dressing to a serving bowl. Toss until well combined. Cover the bowl and chill for 2 hours before serving.

Serve the salad on lettuce leaves if desired.

Chicken Pasta Salad

Makes 6 servings

Ingredients

4 boneless skinless chicken breast, 4 oz. each
3 1/2 cups cooked small pasta shells
3 cups broccoli florets
1 cup red bell pepper, cut into thin strips
6 oz. fresh snow pea pods, trimmed
1/4 cup sliced green onions
1/4 cup vegetable oil
1/4 cup plus 1 tbs. red wine vinegar
2 tbs. honey
2 tsp. toasted sesame seeds
2 garlic cloves, minced
1/2 tsp. ground ginger
1/4 tsp. salt

Directions

In a sauce pan over medium heat, add the chicken. Cover the chicken with water. Cook about 20 minutes or until the chicken is no longer pink and tender. Remove the chicken from the heat and drain all the water from the chicken. Cool the chicken for 15 minutes. Chop the chicken into bite size pieces.

Add the chicken, pasta shells, broccoli, red bell pepper, snow pea pods and green onions to a serving bowl. Toss until combined. In a small bowl, add the vegetable oil, red wine vinegar, honey, sesame seeds, garlic, ginger and salt. Whisk until well combined. Let the dressing sit at room temperature for 5 minutes. Whisk the dressing again.

Pour the dressing over the chicken and vegetables. Toss until well combined. Cover the bowl and chill the salad for 2 hours before serving.

Tarragon Pasta Chicken Salad

Makes 4 servings

Ingredients

8 oz. bottle Italian salad dressing
1/4 cup white wine vinegar
2 tbs. minced fresh tarragon
1 garlic clove, minced
4 boneless skinless chicken breast, about 4 oz. each
4 oz. seashell macaroni
2 cups sliced celery
1/2 cup chopped red bell pepper
1/2 cup chopped green bell pepper
1/4 cup chopped green onions
1/2 cup mayonnaise
1 tbs. chopped fresh parsley

Directions

In a jar with a lid, add the Italian dressing, white wine vinegar, tarragon and garlic. Place the lid on the jar and shake until well combined. Place the chicken in a shallow baking dish. Pour 3/4 cup dressing over the chicken. Cover the dish and refrigerate the chicken for 8 hours. Save the remaining dressing for use later in the recipe.

Remove the chicken from the refrigerator and let the chicken sit at room temperature for 30 minutes. Preheat the oven to 350°. Remove the cover from the chicken. Bake for 25-30 minutes or until the chicken is no longer pink and tender. Remove the chicken from the oven and cool for 10 minutes. Chop the chicken into bite size pieces.

In a large sauce pan over medium heat, add 6 cups water. Bring the water to a boil and add the macaroni. Boil for 6-7 minutes or until the macaroni is tender. Remove the pan from the heat and drain all the water from the macaroni. Rinse the macaroni in cold water and drain all the water again.

Add the macaroni, chicken, remaining dressing, celery, red bell pepper, green bell pepper, green onions, mayonnaise and parsley to a serving bowl. Toss until well combined. Cover the bowl and chill for 4 hours before serving.

Chicken Tortellini Salad

Makes 6 servings

Ingredients

3/4 cup plus 4 tbs. olive oil
2 garlic cloves, minced
1 lb. boneless skinless chicken breast, cut into strips
8 oz. pkg. tortellini with Parmesan
3 celery stalks, chopped
1 red bell pepper, cut into strips
1/3 cup chopped purple onion
5 oz. smoked Gouda, cut into thin strips
3/4 cup cider vinegar
2 tbs. honey
2 tbs. Dijon mustard
12 Bibb lettuce leaves

Directions

In a skillet over medium heat, add 2 tablespoons olive oil, garlic and chicken strips. Saute the chicken for 6-7 minutes or until the chicken is no longer pink and tender. Remove the skillet from the heat and drain the remaining olive oil from the skillet.

In a large sauce pan over medium heat, add 10 cups water. Bring the water to a boil and add the tortellini. Boil for 8-10 minutes or until the tortellini is tender. Remove the pan from the heat and drain all the water from the pasta. Rinse the tortellini in cold water and drain all the water again.

In a large bowl, add 2 tablespoons olive oil and the tortellini. Toss until the tortellini is coated in the olive oil. Add the chicken, celery, red bell pepper, purple onion and Gouda cheese. Toss until combined.

In a mixing bowl, add 3/4 cup olive oil, cider vinegar, honey and Dijon mustard. Whisk until well combined. Pour the dressing over the salad. Toss until combined. You can chill the salad or serve at room temperature.

Place the Bibb lettuce on a serving platter. Spoon the pasta salad over the lettuce and serve.

Ranch Turkey & Pasta Salad

Makes 8 servings

Ingredients

2 cups dry penne pasta
2 cups chopped cooked turkey
1 zucchini, sliced
2 yellow squash, sliced
1 green bell pepper, chopped
1 red bell pepper, chopped
1/4 cup grated Parmesan cheese
1 cup prepared ranch dressing

Directions

In a large sauce pan over medium heat, add 2 quarts water. Bring the water to a boil and add the penne pasta. Boil for 8-9 minutes or until the pasta is tender. Remove the pan from the heat and drain all the water from the pasta. Rinse the pasta with cold water and drain all the water again.

Add the pasta, turkey, zucchini, yellow squash, green bell pepper, red bell pepper, Parmesan cheese and ranch dressing to a large bowl. Toss until well combined. Cover the bowl and chill for 2 hours before serving.

Confetti Tuna Salad

Makes 8 servings

Ingredients

1 cup elbow macaroni
1 1/2 cups chopped celery
12 oz. can tuna, drained and flaked
1/4 cup sliced green olives
2 tbs. chopped green bell pepper
1 tbs. chopped onion
1 cup mayonnaise
Salt and black pepper to taste

Directions

In a large sauce pan over medium heat, add 8 cups water. Bring the water to a boil and add the macaroni. Boil for 6-7 minutes or until the macaroni is tender. Remove the pan from the heat and drain all the water from the macaroni. Rinse the macaroni in cold water and drain all the water again.

Add the macaroni, celery, tuna, green olives, green bell pepper, onion and mayonnaise to a serving bowl. Toss until well combined. Season to taste with salt and black pepper. Cover the bowl and chill for 3 hours before serving.

Gourmet Tuna Pasta Salad

Makes 4 servings

Ingredients

5 oz. bow tie pasta
7 oz. jar marinated hearts of palm, drained
6 oz. jar marinated artichoke hearts, drained
6 oz. can albacore white tuna, drained and flaked
1/2 cup frozen green peas, thawed
1/4 cup pimento stuffed green olives, sliced
1/4 cup sliced black olives
1/4 cup seeded and chopped Greek salad peppers
1/4 cup shredded mozzarella cheese
1/4 cup shredded cheddar cheese
2 tbs. chopped green onion
2 tbs. grated Parmesan cheese
1/2 cup bottled Italian salad dressing
1/8 tsp. black pepper

Directions

In a large sauce pan over medium heat, add 8 cups water. Bring the water to a boil and add the bow tie pasta. Boil for 6-7 minutes or until the pasta is tender. Remove the pan from the heat and drain all the water from the pasta. Rinse the pasta with cold water and drain all the water from the pasta again.

In a large bowl, add the bow tie pasta, hearts of palm, artichoke hearts, tuna, green peas, green olives, black olives, Greek salad peppers, mozzarella cheese, cheddar cheese, green onion, Parmesan cheese, Italian salad dressing and black pepper. Gently toss until well combined. Cover the bowl and chill for 2 hours before serving.

Tuna Macaroni Salad

Makes 4 servings

Ingredients

2 cups cooked elbow macaroni
6 oz. can tuna, drained and flaked
1 hard boiled egg, chopped
1/2 cup cubed cheddar cheese
1/2 cup frozen green peas, thawed
1/2 cup mayonnaise
2 tbs. chopped dill pickle
2 tbs. minced onion

Directions

Add all the ingredients to a serving bowl. Stir until well blended. Cover the bowl and chill for 2 hours before serving.

Stuffed Tomato with Tuna Pasta Salad

Makes 5 servings

Ingredients

1 cup whole wheat shell macaroni
6 oz. can tuna, drained and chilled
3/4 cup thinly sliced carrots
1/2 cup frozen green peas, thawed
1/4 cup chopped celery
1/4 cup chopped cucumber
1/4 cup thinly sliced radishes
1 tbs. minced onion
1/2 cup plain yogurt
2 tbs. Dijon mustard
1 tbs. mayonnaise
1 tbs. vinegar
1/8 tsp. black pepper
5 tomatoes

Directions

In a large sauce pan over medium heat, add 8 cups water. Bring the water to a boil and add the macaroni. Boil for 6-7 minutes or until the macaroni is tender. Remove the pan from the heat and drain all the water from the pan. Rinse the macaroni in cold water and drain all the water again.

In a mixing bowl, add the macaroni, tuna, carrots, green peas, celery, cucumber, radishes and onion. Toss until combined. In a small bowl, add the yogurt, mustard, mayonnaise, vinegar and black pepper. Stir until well combined and add to the salad. Toss until well combined.

Remove the core from the tomatoes. Cut each tomato in 6 wedges. Place each tomato on a serving plate. Spoon the pasta salad over the tomatoes when ready to serve.

Whole Wheat Tuna Macaroni Salad

Makes 6 servings

Ingredients

1 1/2 cups whole wheat seashell macaroni
3 cups fresh broccoli, chopped
1 large tomato, seeded and chopped
2 green onions, thinly sliced
6 oz. can tuna, drained and flaked
1 tbs. chopped fresh basil
1/2 tsp. dried oregano
2 tbs. red wine vinegar
1 tbs. olive oil
1/8 tsp. salt
Black pepper to taste

Directions

In a large sauce pan over medium heat, add 8 cups water. Bring the water to a boil and add the macaroni. Boil for 6-7 minutes or until the macaroni is tender. Remove the pan from the heat and drain all the water from the macaroni. Rinse the macaroni with cold water and drain all the water again.

Add the macaroni, broccoli, tomato, green onions and tuna to a serving bowl. In a jar with a lid, add the basil, oregano, red wine vinegar, olive oil and salt. Place the lid on the jar and shake until well combined. Pour the dressing over the salad. Toss until well combined. Season to taste with black pepper. Serve the salad at room temperature or chilled.

Tuna Vegetable Pasta Salad

Makes 8 servings

Ingredients

6 oz. spinach rotini pasta
1/2 cup sliced green onions
1/2 cup green bell pepper, cut into thin strips
1/2 cup sliced black olives
1 cup cherry tomatoes, halved
1 carrot, shredded
12 oz. can tuna, drained and flaked
1/2 cup vegetable oil
3 tbs. white wine vinegar
2 tbs. lemon juice
3 tbs. minced fresh parsley
1/2 tsp. salt
1/4 tsp. black pepper
1 green onion, cut into 1" pieces
1 garlic clove, halved
Lettuce leaves, optional

Directions

In a large sauce pan over medium heat, add 8 cups water. Bring the water to a boil and add the rotini pasta. Boil for 6-7 minutes or until the pasta is tender. Remove the pan from the heat and drain all the water from the pasta. Rinse the pasta with cold water and drain all the water from the pasta again.

In a mixing bowl, add the pasta, sliced green onions, green bell pepper, black olives, tomatoes, carrot and tuna. Toss until combined.

In a blender, add the vegetable oil, white wine vinegar, lemon juice, parsley, salt, black pepper, cut green onion pieces and garlic. Process until smooth.

Pour the dressing over the salad. Toss until combined. Cover the bowl and chill for 8 hours before serving. Serve the salad over lettuce leaves if desired.

Salmon and Macaroni Salad

Makes 6 servings

Ingredients

15 oz. can salmon, drained
8 oz. pkg. elbow macaroni
1 onion, finely chopped
1 cucumber, sliced
1/4 cup chopped fresh parsley
1/4 cup plus 2 tbs. vegetable oil
2 tbs. vinegar
2 tsp. salt
1/2 tsp. dry mustard
1/4 tsp. black pepper

Directions

Remove the skin and bone from the salmon. In a large sauce pan over medium heat, add 8 cups water. Bring the water to a boil and add the macaroni. Boil for 6-7 minutes or until the macaroni is tender. Remove the pan from the heat and drain all the water from the macaroni. Rinse the macaroni with cold water and drain all the water again.

In a serving bowl, add the macaroni, salmon, onion, cucumber and parsley. In a jar with a lid, add the vegetable oil, vinegar, salt, dry mustard and black pepper. Place the lid on the jar and shake until combined. Pour the dressing over the salad. Toss until well combined. Cover the bowl and chill for 3 hours before serving.

Crab Meat Macaroni Salad

Makes 8 servings

Ingredients

8 oz. pkg. small shell macaroni
6 oz. lump cooked crab meat, diced
1/2 cup chopped celery
1 onion, chopped
2 hard boiled eggs, chopped
3 slices bacon, cooked and crumbled
1/2 cup mayonnaise
1 tbs. sweet pickle relish
1 1/2 tsp. lemon juice
1/2 tsp. salt
1/4 tsp. dried parsley flakes
1/4 tsp. black pepper

Directions

In a large sauce pan over medium heat, add 8 cups water. Bring the water to a boil and add the macaroni. Boil for 6-7 minutes or until the macaroni is tender. Remove the pan from the heat and drain all the water from the macaroni. Rinse the macaroni with cold water and drain all the water again.

Add the macaroni, crab meat, celery, onion, eggs, bacon, mayonnaise, sweet pickle relish, lemon juice, salt, parsley flakes and black pepper to a serving bowl. Stir until well combined. Cover the bowl and chill for 3 hours before serving.

Crab Meat Shrimp Pasta Salad

Makes 6 servings

Ingredients

11 cups water
1 lb. unpeeled fresh shrimp
6 oz. seashell macaroni
1 cup thinly sliced celery
1/2 cup chopped green bell pepper
1/2 cup purple onion, chopped
2 green onions, chopped
1 tbs. minced fresh parsley
1/4 cup mayonnaise
1/4 cup prepared Italian salad dressing
1/2 tsp. dried oregano
1/4 tsp. salt
1/8 tsp. black pepper
8 oz. cooked crab meat, chopped

Directions

In a sauce pan over medium heat, add 3 cups water. When the water comes to a boil, add the shrimp. Cook for 5 minutes or until the shrimp are pink and tender. Remove the pan from the heat and drain all the water from the pan. Rinse the shrimp in cold water and drain the water again. Peel and devein the shrimp. Place the shrimp in a bowl and refrigerate until chilled.

In a large sauce pan over medium heat, add 8 cups water. Bring the water to a boil and add the macaroni. Boil for 6-7 minutes or until the macaroni is tender. Remove the pan from the heat and drain all the water from the macaroni. Rinse the macaroni in cold water and drain all the water again.

Add the macaroni, celery, green bell pepper, purple onion, green onions, parsley, mayonnaise, Italian salad dressing, oregano, salt and black pepper to a serving bowl. Stir until well combined. Add the shrimp and crab meat to the bowl. Gently toss until combined. Cover the bowl and chill for 1 hour before serving.

Shrimp Delight Salad

Makes 10 servings

Ingredients

12 1/2 cups water
1 lb. fresh shrimp
1 lb. pkg. linguine noodles
6 oz. pkg. frozen snow peas, thawed
6 green onions, chopped
4 tomatoes, peeled and chopped
3/4 cup olive oil
1/4 cup minced fresh parsley
1/3 cup wine vinegar
1 tsp. dried oregano
1 1/2 tsp. dried basil
1/2 tsp. garlic salt
1/2 tsp. black pepper

Directions

In a sauce pan over medium heat, add 4 1/2 cups water. When the water comes to a boil, add the shrimp. Cook for 5 minutes or until the shrimp are pink and tender. Remove the pan from the heat and drain all the water from the pan. Rinse the shrimp in cold water and drain the water again. Peel and devein the shrimp. Place the shrimp in a bowl and refrigerate until chilled.

In a large sauce pan over medium heat, add 8 cups water. Bring the water to a boil and add the linguine. Boil for 8 minutes or until the noodles are tender. Remove the pan from the heat and drain all the water from the noodles. Rinse the noodles in cold water and drain all the water again.

Add the noodles, snow peas, green onions, tomatoes, olive oil, parsley, wine vinegar, oregano, basil, garlic salt and black pepper to a serving bowl. Toss until well combined. Add the shrimp and toss until combined. Cover the bowl and chill for 2 hours before serving.

Shrimp Pasta Medley

Makes 6 servings

Ingredients

13 cups water
1 1/2 lbs. fresh shrimp
1 cup dried rotini pasta
6 oz. pkg. frozen green peas, thawed
4 oz. jar button mushrooms, drained
1/2 cup freshly grated Parmesan cheese
1/4 cup thinly sliced celery
1/4 cup pimento stuffed olives
1/4 cup sliced black olives
1 tsp. minced fresh parsley
1 tsp. white wine
8 oz. bottle Italian salad dressing
Lettuce leaves, optional

Directions

In a large sauce pan over medium heat, add 5 cups water. Bring the water to a boil and add the shrimp. Cook for 5 minutes or until the shrimp are pink and tender. Remove the pan from the heat and drain all the water from the shrimp. Rinse the shrimp in cold water to stop the cooking process. Peel and devein the shrimp. Set the shrimp in the refrigerator until chilled. Remove the tails from the shrimp and chop into bite size pieces.

In a large sauce pan over medium heat, add 8 cups water. Bring the water to a boil and add the pasta. Boil for 6-7 minutes or until the pasta is tender. Remove the pan from the heat and drain all the water from the pasta. Rinse the pasta with cold water and drain all the water from the pasta again.

In a large bowl, add the pasta, green peas, mushrooms, Parmesan cheese, celery, pimento stuffed olives, black olives, parsley, white wine and Italian dressing. Toss until well combined. Add the shrimp and toss until combined. Cover the bowl and refrigerate for 2 hours before serving. Serve the salad over lettuce leaves if desired.

Hearty Macaroni Salad

Makes 6 servings

Ingredients

1 cup elbow macaroni
3/4 lb. cooked ham, cut into 1" strips
1 1/2 cups diced sharp cheddar cheese
1 cup chopped celery
1/2 cup chopped onion
1/2 cup chopped sweet pickle
1/2 cup sour cream
2 tbs. yellow prepared mustard

Directions

In a large sauce pan over medium heat, add 8 cups water. Bring the water to a boil and add the macaroni. Boil for 6-7 minutes or until the macaroni is tender. Remove the pan from the heat and drain all the water from the macaroni. Rinse the macaroni with cold water and drain all the water again.

Add the macaroni, ham, cheddar cheese, celery, onion, sweet pickle, sour cream and mustard to a serving bowl. Stir until well combined. Cover the bowl and chill for 2 hours before serving.

Ham Dijon Pasta Salad

Makes 6 servings

Ingredients

7 oz. pkg. refrigerated rigatoni
2 cups cubed cooked ham
1 cup shredded Swiss cheese
1 carrot, thinly sliced
1/2 tsp. black pepper
8 oz. carton plain yogurt
1 tbs. Dijon mustard
Lettuce leaves, optional

Directions

In a large sauce pan over medium heat, add 8 cups water. Bring the water to a boil and add the rigatoni. Boil for 5-6 minutes or until the rigatoni is tender. Remove the pan from the heat and drain all the water from the pasta. Rinse the pasta with cold water and drain all the water from the pasta again.

Add the rigatoni, ham, Swiss cheese, carrot, black pepper, yogurt and Dijon mustard to a large bowl. Toss until well combined. Cover the bowl and chill for 2 hours before serving. Serve the salad on lettuce leaves if desired.

Italian Pasta Vinaigrette

Makes 4 servings

Ingredients

9 oz. pkg. refrigerated cheese ravioli
3 tbs. olive oil
3 tbs. white wine vinegar
1/2 tsp. dried Italian seasoning
1/4 tsp. black pepper
6 cherry tomatoes, halved
1/4 cup sliced green onions
1 cup cubed cooked ham

Directions

In a large sauce pan over medium heat, add 8 cups water. Bring the water to a boil and add the ravioli. Boil for 6-7 minutes or until the ravioli are tender. Remove the pan from the heat and drain all the water from the ravioli. Rinse the ravioli with cold water and drain all the water from the ravioli again.

In a small bowl, whisk together the olive oil, white wine vinegar, Italian seasoning and black pepper. Whisk until well combined. In a large bowl, add the cheese ravioli, tomatoes, green onions and ham. Pour the dressing over the ravioli. Gently toss until combined. Cover the bowl and chill for 3 hours before serving.

Kid Pleasing Ham Pasta Salad

Makes 6 servings

Ingredients

8 oz. shell macaroni
1 cup chopped cooked ham
1/2 cup chopped green bell pepper
1 large tomato, chopped
1/2 cup mayonnaise
1/4 cup freshly grated Parmesan cheese

Directions

In a large sauce pan over medium heat, add 8 cups water. Bring the water to a boil and add the macaroni. Boil for 6-7 minutes or until the macaroni is tender. Remove the pan from the heat and drain all the water from the macaroni. Rinse the macaroni with cold water and drain all the water from the pan again.

In a mixing bowl, add the macaroni, ham, green bell pepper, tomato, mayonnaise and Parmesan cheese. Toss until well combined. Cover the bowl and chill for 2 hours before serving.

Ranch Macaroni Vegetable Salad

Makes 8 servings

Ingredients

1 1/2 cups rotini pasta
2 tomatoes, chopped
1 cup frozen green peas, thawed
8 oz. cooked ham, cut into thin strips
3/4 cup ranch dressing
1/2 cup chopped green bell pepper
1 cup sliced mushrooms

Directions

In a large sauce pan over medium heat, add 8 cups water. Bring the water to a boil and add the pasta. Boil for 6-7 minutes or until the pasta is tender. Remove the pan from the heat and drain all the water from the pasta. Rinse the pasta in cold water and drain all the water again.

Add the pasta, tomatoes, green peas, ham, ranch dressing, green bell pepper and mushrooms to a serving bowl. Toss until combined. Cover the bowl and chill for 3 hours before serving.

Ham Pecan Blue Cheese Pasta Salad

Makes 6 servings

Ingredients

3 cups dry bow tie pasta
4 oz. cooked ham, cut into thin strips
1 cup chopped pecans
4 oz. pkg. crumbled blue cheese
1/2 cup chopped fresh parsley
2 tbs. minced fresh rosemary
1 garlic clove, minced
1/2 tsp. black pepper
1/4 cup olive oil
1/4 cup grated Parmesan cheese

Directions

In a large sauce pan over medium heat, add 8 cups water. Bring the water to a boil and add the bow tie pasta. Boil for 6-7 minutes or until the pasta is tender. Remove the pan from the heat and drain all the water from the pasta. Rinse the pasta with cold water and drain all the water from the pasta again.

Add the pasta, ham, pecans, blue cheese, parsley, rosemary, garlic, black pepper and olive oil to a serving bowl. Toss until well combined. Sprinkle the Parmesan cheese over the top before serving. You can serve the salad chilled or at room temperature.

Rotini Salad

Makes 6 servings

Ingredients

2 1/2 cups dry rotini pasta
1 cup sliced fresh mushrooms
1/2 cup green bell pepper, cut into thin strips
1/2 cup red bell pepper, cut into thin strips
1/4 cup sliced green onions
1/2 cup freshly grated Parmesan cheese
1/2 cup bottled Italian salad dressing
2 tbs. capers
1/4 tsp. black pepper
8 slices bacon, cooked and crumbled

Directions

In a large sauce pan over medium heat, add 8 cups water. Bring the water to a boil and add the pasta. Boil for 6-7 minutes or until the pasta is tender. Remove the pan from the heat and drain all the water from the pasta. Rinse the pasta in cold water and drain all the water again.

Add the rotini pasta, mushrooms, green bell pepper, red bell pepper, green onions, Parmesan cheese, Italian dressing, capers and black pepper to a serving bowl. Stir until combined. Cover the bowl and chill for 1 hour. Stir the bacon into the salad before serving.

Printed in Great Britain
by Amazon